YOUR CRIMINAL JUSTICE CAREER

A Guidebook

YOUR CRIMINAL JUSTICE CAREER

A Guidebook
Second Edition

The Justice Research Association
(with information from the Bureau of Labor Statistics)

Compiled by Frank Schmalleger

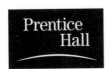

Prentice Hall, Upper Saddle River, New Jersey 07458

Library of Congress Cataloging-in-Publication Data

Your criminal justice career: a guidebook/the Justice Research Association (with information from the Bureau of Labor Statistics); compiled by Frank Schmalleger—2nd ed.
  p. cm.
  Includes index.
  ISBN 0-13-042218-5
  1. Criminal justice, Administration of—Vocational guidance—United States. I. Schmalleger, Frank. II. Justice Research Association. III. United States. Bureau of Labor Statistics.

HV9950 .Y69 2002
364'.023'73—dc21   2001058088

Publisher: Jeff Johnston   **Creative Director:** Cheryl Asherman
Executive Acquisitions Editor: Kim Davies   **Cover Design:** Carey Davies
Assistant Editor: Sarah Holle   **Cover Design Coordinator:** Miguel Ortiz
Managing Editor: Mary Carnis   **Composition:** Janet Bolton
Production Liaison: Barbara Cappuccio   **Copy Editor:** Judith Riotto
Production Editor: Janet Bolton   **Marketing Manager:** Jessica Pfaff
Director of Manufacturing   **Printing and Binding:** Phoenix Book Tech Park
  and Production: Bruce Johnson   **Manufacturing Buyer:** Cathleen Petersen

Pearson Education LTD.
Pearson Education Australia PTY, Limited
Pearson Education Singapore, Pte. Ltd.
Pearson Education North Asia Ltd.
Pearson Education Canada, Ltd.
Pearson Educacion de Mexico, S.A. de C.V.
Pearson Education—Japan
Pearson Education Malaysia, Pte. Ltd.
Pearson Education, Upper Saddle River, New Jersey

10 9 8 7 6 5 4 3 2
ISBN 0-13-042218-5

Contents

Foreword

According to a recent *New York Times* article, the criminal justice field is undergoing explosive growth.[1] The *Times* estimated that in 1998 there were more than 350,000 undergraduate students majoring in criminal justice at the graduate and undergraduate levels in the United States. Add to that the thousands of other students who take criminal justice courses out of curiosity or to fulfill an elective requirement, and the number of students enrolled in such courses in a given year is nothing short of phenomenal.

One reason for the large and rapidly growing cadre of criminal justice majors is a fascination with criminals and with understanding criminal behavior. Popular movies and television shows have piqued the interest of many, leading to a flood of students into criminal justice curricula. But at another level, says the *Times*, "the flood of new courses and students is a reflection of the intellectual success of criminal justice." Many students now entering the justice field are led by personal idealism. They hope to make a difference in the fight against crime and in addressing the conditions that give rise to unlawful behavior.

Fortunately for students in the field, the criminal justice system in this country is growing rapidly, and the job market for criminal justice personnel appears able to accommodate most graduating students for years to come.

This guide is intended to meet the needs of criminal justice students who will soon be entering the job market. It brings

---

[1] Fox Butterfield, "A Newcomer Breaks into the Liberal Arts: Criminal Justice," *New York Times*, December 5, 1998, p. B1.

together, in one convenient place, information from the U.S. Bureau of Labor Statistics (BLS) on criminal justice and public safety occupations. Most of the information contained in this volume comes from the Bureau of Labor Statistics' *2000-2001 Occupational Outlook Handbook*. It has been adapted here to assist college and university criminal justice students preparing for careers in the justice and public safety fields.

The *Occupational Outlook Handbook* is a massive publication that covers employment projections for the nation in great detail and that describes a large number of career areas. Sorting through the *Handbook*, which contains more than a thousand employment categories, and finding material of interest can be a daunting task. Hence it is my hope that this guide will make important BLS information on criminal justice careers readily available to those interested in working in the American justice system and in public safety occupations.

Much of the information contained in this guide is also available at the federal government's *Occupational Outlook Handbook* site on the World Wide Web (http://stats.bls.gov/ocohome.htm). Portions of Chapter 12 come from Frank Schmalleger's *Definitive Guide to Criminal Justice and Criminology on the World Wide Web* (Prentice Hall, 2002).

Thank you for using this guide. If you have any comments or suggestions, please write to me at justice@hargray.com.

Frank Schmalleger, Ph.D., Director,
The Justice Research Association
Professor Emeritus,
The University of North Carolina
at Pembroke

CHAPTER 1

Finding a Job

$\mathcal{S}$ignificant Points

- Choice of employment is one of the most crucial decisions you can make.
- Some of the best employment information is readily available through personal contacts, classified advertisements, public libraries, the World Wide Web, and other easily accessible sources.

/ntroduction

Finding employment (and accepting a job offer) is one of the most crucial decisions you can make. Your choice of careers

The material in this chapter was adapted from Bureau of Labor Statistics, U.S. Department of Labor, *Occupational Outlook Handbook*, 2000-01 Edition, Bulletin 2520. Superintendent of Documents, U.S. Government Printing Office, Washington, D.C., 2000.

is an important determinant of life satisfaction. A job can be rewarding in a number of ways—from the daily personal satisfaction that comes from helping others or from knowing that you are contributing positively to society, to the financial rewards that arrive every week in the form of a paycheck. The reward of knowing that you are helping others is commonly cited by those entering criminal justice and public safety occupations as one reason for their choice of careers.

Salary, of course, is also an important job consideration. But when choosing a job, it is good to keep in mind that the financial benefits of employment extend beyond salary to encompass fringe benefits, including health and retirement plans paid for or sponsored by employers. Such benefits can have a significant impact on your quality of life—especially if you or a family member becomes sick or as retirement time approaches.

For college students, job seeking usually begins in the months immediately prior to graduation. Career experts tell us, however, that the more time you spend considering what kind of job you want, the more likely you are to find satisfying employment.

Sources of Information

What are some of the best sources of information that you can use in finding and choosing a job? According to the 2000-2001 *Occupational Outlook Handbook*, they include personal contacts; classified ads; Internet resources; state employment services; public libraries, career centers, and guidance offices; professional counselors; professional societies, trade associations, labor unions, business firms, and educational institutions; job-matching and referral services; private employment agencies; college career-planning and placement offices; community agencies; employers; and the federal government. The remainder of this chapter discusses each of these sources in some detail.

PERSONAL CONTACTS

Your network of family, friends, and acquaintances may offer one of the most effective ways to find a job. People you know may help you directly or may put you in touch with someone else who can. Networking can introduce you to people who are hiring for their agency or firm or who know of specific job openings.

The people close to you—your family and friends—can be extremely helpful in providing career information. They may be able to answer your questions directly or put you in touch with someone else who can. This type of networking can lead to meeting someone who can answer your questions about a specific career, agency, or company and who can provide inside information and other helpful hints. This is an effective way to learn about the type of training necessary for a certain position, how people in that position entered the field, the prospects for advancement, and what they like and dislike about the work.

CLASSIFIED ADS

The "help wanted" sections in newspapers list hundreds of jobs. You should realize, however, that many other job openings are not listed and that the classified ads sometimes do not give all of the important information. Many offer little or no description of the job, working conditions, or pay. Some ads do not identify the employer. They may simply give a post office box for sending your résumé. This makes follow-up inquiries very difficult. Furthermore, some ads offer out-of-town jobs; others advertise employment agencies rather than actual employment openings.

Keep the following in mind when using classified ads:

- Do not rely solely on the classifieds to find a job; follow other leads as well.
- Answer ads promptly; openings may be filled quickly, even before the ad stops appearing in the paper.

- Read the ads every day, particularly on Sunday, when the most listings usually appear.
- Beware of "no experience necessary" ads. These words often signal low wages, poor working conditions, or commission work.
- Keep a record of all ads to which you respond, including the specific skills, educational background, and personal qualifications required for the position.

INTERNET RESOURCES

A variety of information is available on the Internet, including jobs and job-search resources and techniques. Internet resources are available seven days a week, 24 hours a day.

The growth of online listings has made a wide variety of resources available continuously. Many companies, professional societies, academic institutions, and government agencies maintain online resources or home pages with the latest information on their organization and its activities.

Listings may include information such as government documents, schedules of events, job openings, and even networking contacts. Listings for academic institutions often provide links to career counseling and placement services through career resource centers, as well as information on financing your education. Colleges and universities also offer online guides to campus facilities and admission requirements and procedures.

The Internet provides much of the same information available through libraries, career centers, and guidance offices. However, no single network or resource will contain all desired information, so be prepared to search a variety of different places. As in a library search, look through various lists by field or discipline or by using particular keywords.

When searching employment databases on the Internet, it is sometimes possible to post your résumé online and send it to an employer via electronic mail (e-mail). Some sources provide this service free of charge, but be careful that you will not incur any additional charges for posting or updating your résumé. A good place to start your job search is *America's Job Bank* (http://www.ajb.dni.us/index.html). See Chapter 12 in this guide for a comprehensive listing of job sites on the Web.

STATE EMPLOYMENT SERVICES

State employment services, sometimes called "job services," operate in conjunction with the U.S. Employment Service of the U.S. Department of Labor. About 1,700 local offices help job-seekers find jobs and help employers find qualified workers at no cost to themselves. To find the office nearest you, look in the state government telephone listings under "Job Service" or "Employment."

PUBLIC LIBRARIES, CAREER CENTERS, AND GUIDANCE OFFICES

These institutions maintain a great deal of up-to-date career material. To begin your library search, look at the catalog listings under "Vocations" or "Careers" and then under specific fields. Check the periodicals section, where you will find trade and professional magazines and journals about specific occupations and industries. Familiarize yourself with the concerns and activities of potential employers by skimming their annual reports and the other information they distribute to the public. You can also find occupational information on videocassettes, in kits, and through computerized information systems. Don't forget the librarians; they can be a great source of information and can save you time by directing you to the information you need.

Check your school's career center or guidance office for programs such as individual counseling and testing, guest speakers, field trips, and career days. Also, read through any pamphlets that describe employment. Always assess career guidance materials carefully. Information should be current. Beware of materials that seem to glamorize the occupation, overstate the earnings, or exaggerate the demand for workers.

PROFESSIONAL COUNSELORS

You may wish to seek help from a counselor. These professionals are trained to help you discover your strengths and weaknesses, guide you through an evaluation of your goals and values, and help you determine what you want in a career. The counselor will not tell you what to do but will administer interest inventories and aptitude tests, interpret the results, and help you explore your options. Counselors also may discuss local job markets and the entry requirements and costs of the schools, colleges, or training programs offering preparation for the kind of work that interests you. You can find counselors in

- High school guidance offices
- College career planning and placement offices
- Placement offices in private vocational/technical schools and institutions
- Vocational rehabilitation agencies
- Counseling services offered by community organizations
- Private counseling agencies and private practices
- State employment service offices affiliated with the U.S. Employment Service

Before employing the services of a private counselor or agency, you may want to seek recommendations and check their credentials. The International Association of Counseling Services (IACS) accredits counseling services throughout the country. To receive a listing of accredited services for your region, send a self-addressed, stamped, business-size envelope to

International Association of Counseling Services
101 South Whiting St., Suite 211
Alexandria, VA 22304

The Directory of Counseling Services, an IACS publication providing employment counseling and other assistance, may be available in your library or school career counseling center.

A list of certified career counselors by state can be obtained from

The National Board of Certified Counselors
3 Terrace Way, Suite D
Greensboro, NC 27403-3660
Phone: (910) 547-0607

PROFESSIONAL SOCIETIES, TRADE ASSOCIATIONS, LABOR UNIONS, BUSINESS FIRMS, AND EDUCATIONAL INSTITUTIONS

These organizations provide a variety of free or inexpensive career materials. For information on such organizations, consult directories in your library's reference section. You may want to start with *The Guide to American Directories* or *The Directory of Directories*. Another useful resource is *The Encyclopedia of Associations*, an annual publication listing professional societies, trade associations, labor unions, and fraternal and patriotic organizations.

The National Technical Information Service Audiovisual Center, a central source for audiovisual material produced by the U.S. government, sells material on jobs and careers. For a catalog, contact

National Technical Information Service Audiovisual Center
5285 Port Royal Rd.
Springfield, VA 22161
Phone: (800) 553-6847

For firsthand experience in an occupation, you may wish to work as an intern. Some internships offer academic credit or pay a stipend and can lead to a full-time job after graduation. Check with guidance offices or college career resource centers or directly with employers for opportunities.

JOB-MATCHING AND REFERRAL SERVICES

At the state employment service office, an interviewer can determine if you are "job ready" or if counseling and testing services would be helpful first. After you are "job ready," you may examine available job listings and select openings that interest you. A staff member can then describe the job openings in detail and arrange for interviews with prospective employers. Employment counselors can arrange for tests to assess your occupational aptitudes and interests. They will also help you choose and prepare for a career.

America's Job Bank, run by the U.S. Department of Labor's Employment and Training Administration, provides information on preparing your résumé and using the Internet for your job search; describes trends in the U.S. job market and state occupational projections; and lists approximately 500,000 job openings on any given day. A wide range of jobs are listed all over the country, and most are full-time jobs in the private sector. Job-seekers can access these listings through the Internet; computers with access to the Internet are available to the public in public employment service offices, as well as in schools, libraries, and several hundred military installations.

Tips for Finding the Right Job, a U.S. Department of Labor pamphlet, offers advice on determining your job skills, organizing your job search, writing a résumé, and making the most of an interview. *Job Search Guide: Strategies for Professionals*, another U.S. Department of Labor publication, discusses specific steps that job-seekers can follow to identify employment opportunities. This publication includes sections on such things as handling job loss, managing personal resources, assessing personal skills and interests, researching the job market, conducting the job search, and networking. Check with your state employment service office, or order a copy of these publications from the U.S. Government Printing Office's Superintendent of Documents. Call (202) 512-1800 for price and ordering information.

PRIVATE EMPLOYMENT AGENCIES

These agencies can be helpful, but they are in business to make money. Most agencies operate on a commission basis, with the fee equal to a percentage of the salary paid to a successful applicant. You or the employer will have to pay this, usually sizable, fee. Find out the exact cost and who is responsible for paying it before using the service.

While employment agencies can help you save time and contact employers who might otherwise be difficult to locate, the costs may outweigh the benefits if you are responsible for the fee. Consider any guarantee the agency offers when considering the cost.

COLLEGE CAREER-PLANNING AND PLACEMENT OFFICES

College placement offices match job openings with their students and alumni. Job-seekers set up appointments and use the facilities for interviews with recruiters. Placement offices usually list part-time, temporary, and summer jobs offered on campus. They also list jobs in regional business, nonprofit, and government organizations. Students can receive career counseling and testing, job-search advice, and use of the career resource library. Here you may attend workshops on such topics as job-search strategy, résumé writing, letter writing, and effective interviewing; have drafts of your résumé critiqued and watch videotapes of mock interviews; explore files of résumés and references; and attend job fairs conducted by the office.

COMMUNITY AGENCIES

Many nonprofit organizations, including churches and synagogues, and vocational rehabilitation agencies, offer counseling, career development, and job-placement services, generally targeted to a particular group, such as women, youth, minorities, ex-offenders, or older workers.

EMPLOYERS

It is possible to apply directly to employers without a referral. You may locate a potential employer in the yellow pages, in directories of local chambers of commerce, and in other directories that provide information about employers. When you find an employer that interests you, you can send a cover letter and résumé even if you are not certain that an opening exists.

THE FEDERAL GOVERNMENT

Information on getting a job with the federal government is available from the Office of Personnel Management through a telephone-based system. Consult your telephone directory under "U.S. Government" for a local number, or call (912) 757-3000; TDD (912) 744-2299. Information is also available from the Office of Personnel Management's Internet site: http://www.usajobs.opm.gov.

CHAPTER 2

Applying for a Job

$\mathcal{S}$ignificant Points

- Most jobs require that you complete and submit an application form or a résumé, along with a cover letter explaining why you are interested in the position and how you qualify for it.
- The cover letter is a way to introduce yourself to a potential employer. It should be written carefully.
- The job interview gives you an excellent opportunity to showcase your qualifications.
- You should prepare carefully for a job interview since it is often the final factor in the employer's decision-making process.

The material in this chapter is adapted from Bureau of Labor Statistics, U.S. Department of Labor, *Occupational Outlook Handbook*, 2000-01 Edition, Bulletin 2520. Superintendent of Documents, U.S. Government Printing Office, Washington, D.C., 2000.

*I*ntroduction

This chapter discusses résumés and application forms, cover letters, and employment interviews—all of which are important components of the job-application process. Although the material covered in this chapter is general, it is as applicable to jobs in the criminal justice and public safety fields as it is to other types of employment.

*R*ésumés and Application Forms

Résumés and application forms are two ways to provide employers with written evidence of your qualifications and skills. Most information appears on both the résumé and the application form, but the way it is presented differs. Some employers prefer a résumé, while others require an application form. The following section presents the basic information you should include in your résumé.

There are many ways of organizing a résumé. Depending on the job, you should choose the format that best highlights your skills, training, and experience. It may be helpful to look in a variety of books and publications in your local library or bookstore for different examples.

WHAT GOES INTO A RÉSUMÉ?

- Name, address, and telephone number
- Employment objective—the type of work or specific job you are seeking
- Education, including school name and address, dates of attendance, curriculum, and highest grade completed or degree awarded
- Experience, paid or volunteer. Include the following for each job: job title, name and location of employer, and dates of employment. Briefly describe your job duties.

- Special skills, proficiency in foreign languages, achievements, membership in organizations, and volunteer work. Note on your résumé, "References available upon request."

Cover Letters

A cover letter is sent with a résumé or application form as a way to introduce yourself to a potential employer. A well-written letter captures the employer's attention, follows the standard business letter format, and includes the following information:

- The name and address of the specific person to whom the letter is addressed
- The reason for your interest in the agency, company, or position
- Your main qualifications for the position (in brief)
- A request for an interview
- Your home and work phone numbers

Interviewing

An interview gives you the opportunity to showcase your qualifications to an employer, so it pays to be well prepared. The information that follows provides some helpful hints.

JOB INTERVIEW TIPS

Preparation
- Learn about the organization.
- Have a specific job or jobs in mind.
- Review your qualifications for the job.

- Prepare answers to broad questions about yourself.
- Review your résumé.
- Practice an interview with a friend or relative.
- Arrive before the scheduled time of your interview.

Personal Appearance
- Be well groomed.
- Dress appropriately.
- Do not chew gum or smoke.

The Interview
- Relax and answer each question concisely.
- Respond promptly.
- Use good manners.
- Learn the name of your interviewer, and shake hands as you meet.
- Use proper English, and avoid slang.
- Be cooperative and enthusiastic.
- Ask questions about the position and the organization.
- Thank the interviewer, and follow up with a letter.

The Test (If the Employer Gives One)

- Listen closely to the instructions.
- Read each question carefully.
- Write legibly and clearly.
- Budget your time wisely, and don't dwell on any one question.

Information to Bring to an Interview

- *Social Security number.*
- *Driver's license number.*
- *Résumé.* Although not all employers require applicants to bring a résumé, you should be able to give the interviewer information about your education, training, and previous employment.
- *References.* Employers usually require three references. Get permission from people before using their names, and make sure they will give you a good reference. Try to avoid listing relatives as your references.

CHAPTER 3

Evaluating a Job Offer

Significant Points

- When you receive a job offer, evaluate it carefully.
- Knowing what you want and expect from a job will help you decide whether to accept the offer.
- Researching potential employers before applying for a position or before accepting an offer of employment helps ensure that you will be satisfied after you start working.

Introduction

Once you receive a job offer, you are faced with a difficult decision and must evaluate the offer carefully. Fortunately,

The material in this chapter is adapted from Bureau of Labor Statistics, U.S. Department of Labor, *Occupational Outlook Handbook*, 2000-01 Edition, Bulletin 2520. Superintendent of Documents, U.S. Government Printing Office, Washington, D.C., 2000.

most organizations will not expect you to accept or reject an offer immediately.

There are many issues to consider when assessing a job offer. Will the agency or organization be a good place to work? Will the job be interesting? How are opportunities for advancement? Is the salary fair? Does the employer offer good benefits?

If you have not already figured out exactly what you want, the following discussion may help you develop a set of criteria for judging job offers, whether you are starting a career, reentering the labor force after a long absence, or planning a career change. The information presented here is not specific to criminal justice and public safety careers, but it is applicable to most professions. This chapter discusses some of the things you should consider when evaluating a job offer.

*T*he Organization

Background information on an organization can help you decide whether it would be a good place for you to work. Factors to consider include the organization's business or activity, financial condition, age, size, and location.

You can generally get background information on an organization, particularly a large organization, by telephoning its public relations office. A public company's annual report to the stockholders tells about its corporate philosophy, history, products or services, goals, and financial status. Most large government agencies, including criminal justice agencies, publish annual reports, and smaller ones can furnish printed materials that describe their programs and missions. Press releases, company and agency newsletters or magazines, and recruitment brochures can also be useful. Ask the agency or organization for any other items that might interest a prospective employee.

If possible, speak to current or former employees of the organization. Background information on the organization also may be available on the Internet or at your public or school library. If you cannot get an annual report, check the library for reference directories that provide basic facts about the agency or company, such as its purpose or function, orientation, products, organizational philosophy, and number of employees.

Stories about an agency or organization can often be found in magazines and newspapers and can tell a great deal about its successes, failures, and plans for the future. You can identify articles on an agency or company by looking under its name in periodical or computerized indexes. However, it may not be useful to look back more than two or three years.

Career centers at colleges and universities often have information on employers that is not available in libraries. Ask a career center representative how to find out about a particular organization. The career center may have an entire file of information on the employer. Things to consider might include the following:

- *Is the organization's business or activity in keeping with your own interests and beliefs?* It will be easier to apply yourself to your work if you are enthusiastic about what the organization does.
- *How will the size of the organization affect you?* Large organizations generally offer a greater variety of training programs and career paths, more managerial levels for advancement, and better employee benefits than small organizations. Large employers may also have more advanced technologies. However, jobs in large agencies or companies may tend to be highly specialized. Jobs in small agencies or small firms may offer broader authority and responsibility, a closer working relationship with top management, and a chance to clearly see your contribution to the success of the organization.
- *Does it make any difference to you whether the employer is a public agency or a private company?* A privately owned company may be controlled by an individual or a family, which can mean that key jobs are reserved for relatives and friends. A publicly owned company is controlled by a board of directors responsible to the stockholders. A pub-

lic agency, like a law enforcement agency, is similar to a publicly owned company in that key jobs are open to anyone with talent.

*T*he Nature of the Job

Even if everything else about the job is good, you will be unhappy if you dislike the day-to-day work. Determining in advance whether you will like the work may be difficult. However, the more you find out about it before accepting or rejecting the job offer, the more likely you are to make the right choice. Actually working in the industry and, if possible, for the agency or company would provide considerable insight. You can gain work experience through part-time, temporary, or summer jobs or through work-study programs and internships while in school, all of which can lead to permanent job offers. You might want to consider the following:

- *Where is the job located?* If it is in another section of the country, you need to consider the cost of living, the availability of housing and transportation, and the quality of educational and recreational facilities in the new location. Even if the job is in your area, consider the time and expense of commuting in your decision.

- *Does the work match your interests and make good use of your skills?* The duties and responsibilities of the job should be explained in enough detail to answer this question.

- *Are you comfortable with the hours?* Most jobs involve regular hours—for example, 40 hours a week, during the day, Monday through Friday. Other jobs, especially those in law enforcement and correctional agencies, require night, weekend, or holiday work. In addition, some jobs routinely require overtime to meet deadlines or sales or production goals or to better serve customers. Consider the effect of work hours on your personal life.

• *How long do most people who enter this job stay with the agency or company?* High turnover can mean dissatisfaction with the nature of the work or something else about the job.

Opportunities Offered by the Employer

A good job offers you opportunities to learn new skills, increase your earnings, and rise to positions of greater authority, responsibility, and prestige. A lack of opportunities can dampen your interest in the work and can lead to frustration and boredom. The company should have a training plan for you. What valuable new skills does the agency or company plan to teach you? The employer should give you some idea of promotion possibilities within the organization. What is the next step on the career ladder? If you have to wait for a job to become vacant before you can be promoted, how long does this usually take? Employers differ on their policies regarding promotion from within the organization. When opportunities for advancement do arise, will you compete with applicants from outside the company? Can you apply for jobs for which you qualify elsewhere within the organization, or is mobility within the organization limited?

Salaries and Benefits

Wait for the employer to introduce these subjects. Some employers will not talk about pay until they have decided to hire you. To know if an offer is reasonable, you need a rough estimate of what the job should pay. You may have to go to several sources for this information. Try to find family, friends, or acquaintances who were recently hired in similar jobs. Ask your teachers and the staff in the college placement office about starting pay for graduates with your qualifications. "Help wanted" ads in newspapers sometimes give salary ranges for similar positions.

If you are considering the salary and benefits for a job in another geographic area, make allowances for differences in the cost of living, which may be significantly higher in a large metropolitan area than in a smaller city, town, or rural area.

You also should learn the organization's policy regarding overtime. Depending on the job, you may be exempt from laws requiring the employer to compensate you for overtime. Find out how many hours you will be expected to work each week and whether you will receive overtime pay or compensatory time off for working more hours.

Also take into account that the starting salary is just that, the start. Your salary should be reviewed on a regular basis; many organizations do it every year. How much can you expect to earn after one, two, three, or more years? An employer cannot be specific about the amount of pay if it includes commissions and bonuses.

Benefits can also add a lot to your base pay, but they vary widely. Find out exactly what the benefit package includes and how much of the cost you must bear.

Check the library or your school's career center for salary surveys, such as those conducted by the National Association of Colleges and Employers or various professional associations.

Data on wages and benefits are also available from

Bureau of Labor Statistics
Office of Compensation and Working Conditions
2 Massachusetts Ave. N.E., Room 4160
Washington, D.C. 20212-0001
Phone: (202) 606-6225

Data from the National Compensation Survey, which integrates data from three existing Bureau of Labor Statistics (BLS) programs—the Employment Cost Index, the Occupational Compensation Survey, and the Employee Benefits Survey—are available from the BLS office and from the Internet (http://stats.bls.gov/comhome.htm).

Current Population Survey (CPS) data on median weekly earnings of full-time wage and salary workers, by detailed occupation, are available from

Bureau of Labor Statistics
Office of Employment and Unemployment Statistics
2 Massachusetts Ave. N.E., Room 4945
Washington, D.C. 20212-0001
Phone: (202) 606-6400

CPS data can also be accessed on the Internet (http://stats.bls.gov/cpsaatab.htm).

CHAPTER 4

Working as an Attorney

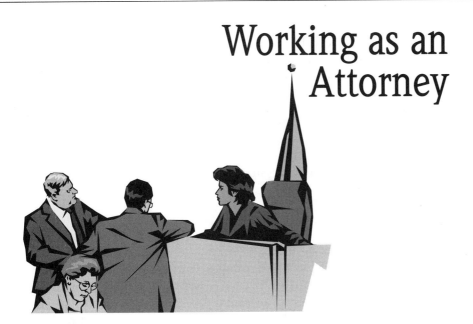

*S*ignificant Points

- There are about 622,000 attorneys practicing law in the United States, and another 78,000 judges.
- Formal educational requirements for the practice of law usually include a four-year college degree, followed by three years in law school. After that, all states require applicants for admission to the bar to pass a written bar examination.
- Aspiring lawyers and judges will encounter significant competition for jobs.
- Competition for admission to many law schools is intense, as the number of applicants greatly exceeds the number that can be admitted.

The material in this chapter is adapted from Bureau of Labor Statistics, U.S. Department of Labor, *Occupational Outlook Handbook*, 2000-01 Edition, Bulletin 2520. Superintendent of Documents, U.S. Government Printing Office, Washington, D.C., 2000.

• Although the job market for lawyers expanded rapidly from 1970 to 1990, opportunities are now more limited. The number of law school graduates is expected to continue to strain the economy's capacity to absorb them.

Nature of the Work

LAWYERS

Lawyers, also called "attorneys," act as both advocates and advisers in our society. As advocates, they represent one of the parties in criminal and civil trials by presenting evidence in court supporting their client. As advisers, lawyers counsel their clients as to their legal rights and obligations, and they suggest particular courses of action in business and personal matters. Whether acting as advocates or advisers, all attorneys interpret the law and apply it to specific situations.

Lawyers research the purposes behind laws and judicial decisions that have been applied to circumstances similar to those that their clients face. While all lawyers continue to use law libraries to prepare cases, some supplement their search of conventional printed sources with computer sources. Software can be used to search legal literature automatically and to identify legal texts relevant to a specific case. In litigation involving many supporting documents, lawyers may use computers to organize and index material. Tax lawyers use computers to make tax computations and to explore alternative tax strategies for their clients.

Lawyers increasingly use the Internet for research and to advertise their services. Ethical standards for advertising on the Internet are still evolving. Lawyers also use electronic filing, videoconferencing, and voice-recognition technology. Electronic filing promotes the sharing of information by providing all parties in a case access to a database with all official filings, briefs, and other court documents. Electronic filing and other new technologies save time and reduce legal costs.

Lawyers communicate the information obtained through research to others. They advise clients and draw up legal documents, such as wills and contracts. Lawyers may not disclose matters discussed in confidence with their clients. They hold positions of great responsibility and are obligated to adhere to a strict code of ethics.

The more detailed aspects of a lawyer's job depend upon his or her field of specialization and position. While all lawyers are licensed to represent parties in court, some appear in court more frequently than others; these lawyers specialize in trial work. Their ability to think quickly and to speak with ease and authority and their familiarity with courtroom rules and strategy are particularly important in trial work. However, trial lawyers still spend most of their time outside the courtroom, conducting research, interviewing clients and witnesses, and handling other details in preparation for trial.

Besides trials, lawyers may specialize in other areas, such as bankruptcy, probate, and international law. Environmental lawyers, for example, may represent public interest groups, waste-disposal companies, or construction firms in their dealings with the Environmental Protection Agency (EPA) and other state and federal agencies. They help their clients prepare and file for licenses and applications for approval before certain activities may occur. They also represent their clients' interests in administrative adjudications.

Some lawyers concentrate in the growing field of intellectual property. These lawyers help protect their clients' claims to copyrights, artwork under contract, product designs, and computer programs. Still other lawyers advise insurance companies about the legality of insurance transactions. They write insurance policies to conform with the law and to protect companies from unwarranted claims. They review claims filed against insurance companies and represent the companies in court.

The majority of lawyers are in private practice, where they concentrate on criminal or civil law. In criminal law, lawyers represent individuals who have been charged with crimes, arguing their cases in courts of law. In civil law, attorneys assist clients with litigation, wills, trusts, contracts, mortgages, titles, and leases. Others handle only public interest cases—civil or criminal—which may have a potential impact extending well beyond the individual client.

Lawyers are sometimes employed full-time by a single client. If the client is a corporation, the lawyer is known as "house counsel" and usually advises the company concerning legal issues related to its business activities. These issues might involve patents, government regulations, contracts with other companies, property interests, or collective bargaining agreements with unions.

A significant number of attorneys are employed at the various levels of government. Lawyers who work for state attorneys general, prosecutors, public defenders, and courts play a key role in the criminal justice system. At the federal level, attorneys investigate cases for the Department of Justice and other agencies. Government lawyers also help develop programs, draft and interpret laws and legislation, establish enforcement procedures, and argue civil and criminal cases on behalf of the government.

Other lawyers work for legal aid societies—private, nonprofit organizations established to serve disadvantaged people. These lawyers generally handle civil, rather than criminal, cases.

A relatively small number of trained attorneys work in law schools. Most are faculty members who specialize in one or more subjects, and others serve as administrators. Some work full-time in nonacademic settings and teach part-time. Some lawyers become judges.

JUDGES

Judges apply the law and oversee the legal process in courts according to local, state, and federal statutes. They preside over cases concerning every aspect of society, from traffic offenses to disputes over management of professional sports, or from the rights of huge corporations to questions of disconnecting life-support equipment for the terminally ill. They must ensure that trials and hearings are conducted fairly and that the court administers justice so as to safeguard the legal rights of all parties involved.

Judges preside over trials or hearings and listen as attorneys representing the parties present and argue their cases. They rule on the admissibility of evidence and the methods of presenting testimony, and they settle disputes between the opposing attorneys. They ensure that rules and procedures are followed, and if unusual circumstances arise for which standard procedures have not been established, judges direct how the trial will proceed based on their knowledge of the law.

Judges often hold pretrial hearings for cases. They listen to allegations and, based on the evidence presented, determine whether there is enough merit for a trial to be held. In criminal cases, judges may decide that the defendants charged with crimes should be held in jail pending their trial, or they may set conditions for release through the trial. In civil cases, judges may impose restrictions upon the parties until a trial is held.

When trials are held, juries are often selected to decide cases, including guilt or innocence in criminal cases and the liability and the amount of compensation in civil cases. In these cases, judges instruct juries on applicable laws, direct them to deduce the facts from the evidence presented, and hear their verdict. However, judges decide cases when the law does not require a jury trial and when the parties waive their right to a jury. In the absence of a jury, the judge determines guilt and imposes sentences in a criminal case; in civil cases, the judge awards relief—such as compensation for damages—to the litigants (the parties in the lawsuit).

Judges also work outside the courtroom "in chambers." In their private office, judges read documents on pleadings and motions, research legal issues, write opinions, and oversee their court's operations. Running a court is like running a small business, and judges also manage their court's administrative and clerical staff.

Judges' duties vary according to the extent of their jurisdiction and power. *General trial court judges* of the federal and state court systems have jurisdiction over any case in their system. They generally try civil cases transcending the jurisdiction of lower courts, as well as all cases involving felony offenses. Federal and state *appellate court judges*, although few in number, have the power to overrule decisions made by trial court or administrative law judges if they determine that legal errors were made in a case or if legal precedent does not support the judgment of the lower court. They rule on fewer cases and rarely have direct contact with litigants. Instead, they usually base their decisions on lower court records and written and oral arguments by lawyers.

Many state court judges preside in courts in which jurisdiction is limited by law to certain types of cases. A variety of titles are assigned to these judges, but among the most common are *municipal court judge, county court judge, magistrate,* and *justice of the peace*. Traffic violations, misdemeanors, small claims cases, and pretrial hearings constitute the bulk of the work of these judges, but some states allow them to handle cases involving domestic relations, probate, contracts, and other selected areas of the law.

Administrative law judges, formerly called *hearing officers*, are employed by government agencies to make determinations for administrative agencies. They make decisions on a person's eligibility for Social Security benefits or workers' compensation, protection of the environment, enforcement of health and safety regulations, employment discrimination, and compliance with economic regulatory requirements.

Working Conditions

Lawyers and judges do most of their work in offices, law libraries, and courtrooms. Lawyers sometimes meet in clients' homes or places of business and, when necessary, in hospitals or prisons. They may travel to attend meetings, gather evidence, and appear before courts, legislative bodies, and other authorities.

Salaried lawyers generally have structured work schedules. Lawyers in private practice may work irregular hours while conducting research, conferring with clients, or preparing briefs. Lawyers often work long hours, and about half regularly work 50 hours or more per week. They are under particularly heavy pressure, for example, when a case is being tried. Preparation for court includes keeping abreast of the latest laws and judicial decisions.

Although legal work is not generally seasonal, the work of tax lawyers and other specialists may be an exception. Lawyers in private practice can often determine their own workload and when they will retire, and many stay in practice well beyond the usual retirement age.

Many judges work a standard 40-hour week, but a third of all judges work over 50 hours per week. Some judges with limited jurisdiction are employed part-time and divide their time between their judicial responsibilities and other careers.

Employment

Lawyers held about 681,000 jobs in 1998; judges, magistrates, and other judicial workers held about 71,000. About seven out of 10 lawyers practiced privately, either in law firms or in solo practices. Most of the remaining lawyers held positions in government, the greatest number at the local level. In the federal government, lawyers work for many different agencies but are concentrated in the Departments of Justice, Treasury, and Defense. Other lawyers are employed as house counsel by public utilities, banks, insurance companies, real estate agencies, manufacturing firms, welfare and religious organizations, and other business firms and nonprofit organizations. Some salaried lawyers also have part-time independent practices; others work as lawyers part-time while working full-time in another occupation.

All judges, magistrates, and other judicial workers are employed by federal, state, or local governments, with about four out of 10 holding positions in the federal government.

Law professors—as well as other professionals such as politicians, managers, and administrators—also hold law degrees.

*T*raining, Other Qualifications, and Advancement

LAWYERS

To practice law in the courts of any state or other jurisdiction, a person must be licensed, or admitted to the bar, under rules established by the jurisdiction's highest court. All require that applicants for admission to the bar pass a written bar examination; most jurisdictions also require applicants to pass a separate written ethics examination. Lawyers who have been admitted to the bar in one jurisdiction may occasionally be admitted to the bar in another without taking an examination if they meet that jurisdiction's standards of good moral character and have a specified amount of legal experience. Federal courts and agencies set their own qualifications for those practicing before them.

To qualify for the bar examination in most states, an applicant must usually obtain a college degree and must graduate from a law school accredited by the American Bar Association (ABA) or the proper state authorities. (ABA accreditation signifies that the law school—particularly its library and faculty—meets certain standards developed to promote quality legal education.) The ABA currently accredits 179 law schools. Others are approved by state authorities only. With certain exceptions, graduates of schools not approved by the ABA are restricted to taking the bar examination and practicing in the state or other jurisdiction in which the school is located; most of these schools are in California. In 1997, seven states accepted the study of law in a law office or in combination with study in a law school; only California accepts the study of law by correspondence as qualification for taking the bar examination. Several states require registration and approval of students by the state board of law examiners, either before they enter law school or during the early years of legal study.

Although there is no nationwide bar examination, 47 states, the District of Columbia, Guam, the Northern Mariana Islands, and the Virgin Islands require the six-hour Multistate Bar Examination (MBE) as part of the bar examination for their jurisdiction. The MBE is not required in Indiana, Louisiana, Washington, and Puerto Rico. The MBE covers issues of broad interest and is sometimes given in addition to a locally prepared state bar examination. The three-hour Multistate Essay Examination (MEE) is used as part of the state bar examination in a few states. States vary in their use of MBE and MEE scores.

Eight states require performance examinations that test the practical skills of beginning lawyers. This examination has been well received, and more states are expected to require performance testing in the future. Requirements vary by state, although the test usually is taken at the same time as the bar exam and is a one-time requirement.

The required college and law school education usually takes seven years of full-time study after high school—four years of undergraduate study followed by three years in law school. Although some law schools accept a very small number of students after three years of college, most require applicants to have a bachelor's degree. To meet the needs of students who can attend only part-time, a number of law schools have night or part-time divisions which usually require four years of study; about one in 10 graduates from ABA-approved schools attends part-time.

Although there is no recommended "prelaw" major, prospective lawyers should develop proficiency in writing and speaking, reading, researching, analyzing, and thinking logically—skills needed to succeed both in law school and in the profession. Whatever the major, a multidisciplinary background is recommended. Courses in English, foreign language, public speaking, government, philosophy, history, economics, mathematics, and computer science, among others, are useful.

Students interested in a particular aspect of law may find related courses helpful. For example, prospective patent lawyers need a strong background in engineering or science, and future tax lawyers must have extensive knowledge of accounting.

Acceptance by most law schools depends on the applicant's ability to demonstrate an aptitude for the study of law, usually through good undergraduate grades, the Law School Admission Test (LSAT), the quality of the applicant's undergraduate school, prior work experience, and sometimes a personal interview. However, law schools vary in the weight they place on each of these and other factors.

All law schools approved by the ABA, except for those in Puerto Rico, require applicants to take the LSAT. Nearly all law schools require applicants to have certified transcripts sent to the Law School Data Assembly Service, which then sends applicants' LSAT scores and their standardized records of college grades to the law schools of their choice. Both this service and the LSAT are administered by the Law School Admission Council.

Competition for admission to many law schools is intense. Enrollment in these schools rose very rapidly during the 1970s, with applicants far outnumbering available seats. The number of applicants decreased markedly in the 1990s, easing competition slightly. However, the number of applicants to most law schools still greatly exceeds the number that can be admitted. Competition for admission to the more prestigious law schools is always keen.

During the first year or year and a half of law school, students generally study fundamental courses such as constitutional law, contracts, property law, torts, civil procedure, and legal writing. In the remaining time, they may elect specialized courses in fields such as tax, labor, and corporation law. Law students often acquire practical experience through participation in school-sponsored legal clinic activities, in the school's moot court competitions in which students conduct appellate arguments, in practice trials under the supervision of experienced lawyers and judges, and through research and writing on legal issues for the school's law journal.

In 1997, law students in 52 U.S. jurisdictions were required to pass the Multistate Professional Responsibility Examination (MPRE), which tests their knowledge of the ABA codes on professional responsibility and judicial conduct. In some states, the MPRE may be taken during law school, usually after completing a course on legal ethics.

A number of law schools have clinical programs in which students gain legal experience through practice trials and law school projects under the supervision of practicing lawyers and law school faculty. Law school clinical programs might include work in legal aid clinics, for example, or on the staff of legislative committees. Part-time or summer clerkships in law firms, government agencies, and corporate legal departments also provide valuable experience. Such training can provide references, can lead directly to a job after graduation, and can help students decide what kind of practice best suits them. Clerkships may also be an important source of financial aid.

Graduates receive the degree of juris doctor (J.D.) as the first professional degree. Advanced law degrees may be desirable for those planning to specialize, do research, or teach. Some law students pursue joint degree programs, which generally require an additional semester or year. Joint degree programs are offered in a number of areas, including law and business administration or public administration.

After graduation, lawyers must stay informed about legal and nonlegal developments that affect their practice. Currently, 39 states and jurisdictions mandate Continuing Legal Education (CLE). Many law schools and state and local bar associations provide continuing education courses that help lawyers stay abreast of recent developments. Some states allow CLE credits to be obtained through participation in seminars on the Internet.

The practice of law involves a great deal of responsibility. Individuals planning careers in law should like to work with people and be able to win the respect and confidence of their clients, their associates, and the public. Perseverance and reasoning ability are essential for analyzing complex cases and reaching sound conclusions. Lawyers also need creativity when handling new and unique legal problems.

Most beginning lawyers start in salaried positions. Newly hired salaried attorneys usually start as associates and work with more experienced lawyers or judges. After several years of progressively more responsible salaried employment, some lawyers are admitted to partnership in their firm or go into practice for themselves. Some lawyers, after several years of practice, become full-time law school faculty or administrators; a growing number have advanced degrees in other fields as well.

Some attorneys use their legal training in administrative or managerial positions in various departments of large corporations. A transfer from a corporation's legal department to another department is often viewed as a way to gain administrative experience and to rise in the ranks of management.

JUDGES

Most judges have first been lawyers. Federal and state judges are generally required to be lawyers. About 40 states allow nonlawyers to hold limited-jurisdiction judgeships, but opportunities are better for those with law experience. Federal administrative law judges must be lawyers and must pass a competitive examination administered by the U.S. Office of Personnel Management. Some state administrative law judges and other hearing officials need not be lawyers, but law degrees are preferred for most positions.

Federal judges are appointed for life by the president, with the consent of the Senate. Federal administrative law judges are appointed by the various federal agencies with virtually lifetime tenure. About half of all state judges are appointed, while the remainder are elected in partisan or nonpartisan state elections. Many state and local judges serve fixed renewable terms, which range from four or six years for some trial court judgeships to as long as 14 years or life for other trial or appellate court judgeships. Judicial nominating commissions, composed of members of the bar and the public, screen candidates for judgeships in many states, as well as in some federal jurisdictions.

All states have some type of orientation for newly elected or appointed judges. The Federal Judicial Center, the ABA, the National Judicial College, and the National Center for State Courts provide judicial education and training for judges and other judicial branch personnel. General and continuing education courses usually run from a couple of days to three weeks. Over half of the states and Puerto Rico require judges to enroll in continuing education courses while serving on the bench.

Job Outlook

Individuals interested in pursuing a career as a lawyer or a judge will encounter keen competition through the year 2008. The number of law school graduates is expected to continue to strain the economy's capacity to absorb them. As for judges, the prestige associated with serving on the bench should ensure continued, intense competition for openings.

LAWYERS

The employment of lawyers grew very rapidly from the early 1970s through the early 1990s but has started to level off in the last several years. Employment is expected to grow about as fast as the average for all occupations through the year 2008. Continuing demand for lawyers will result from growth in the population and the general level of business activities. Demand will also be spurred by growth of legal action in such areas as health care, intellectual property, international law, elder law, sexual harassment, and the environment. The wider availability and affordability of legal clinics and prepaid legal service programs should result in the increased use of legal services by middle-income people.

Employment growth will be slower than in the past. In an effort to reduce the money spent on legal fees, many businesses are turning to large accounting firms to provide employee benefit counseling, to process documents, and to handle other services previously performed by law firms. Also, mediation and dispute resolution are increasingly used as alternatives to litigation.

Competition for job openings will continue to be keen because of the large numbers graduating from law school each year. During the 1970s, the annual number of law school graduates more than doubled, outpacing the rapid growth of jobs. Growth in the yearly number of law school graduates slowed during the early to mid-1980s but increased again in the late 1980s to early 1990s. Although graduates with superior academic records from well-regarded law schools will have more job opportunities, most graduates will encounter stiff competition for jobs. As in the past, some graduates may have to accept positions in areas outside their field of interest or for which they are overqualified. They may choose to enter jobs for which legal training is an asset but not normally a requirement—for example, administrative, managerial, and business positions in banks, insurance firms, real estate companies, government agencies, and other organizations.

Some recent law school graduates who are unable to find permanent positions are turning to the growing number of legal temporary staffing firms, which place attorneys in short-term jobs until they are able to secure full-time positions. This service allows companies to hire lawyers on an "as needed" basis and allows beginning lawyers to develop practical skills while looking for permanent positions.

In times of high competition for jobs, a law graduate's geographic mobility and work experience assume greater importance. The willingness to relocate may be an advantage in getting a job, but to be licensed in a new state, a lawyer may have to take an additional state bar examination. In addition, employers increasingly seek graduates who have advanced law degrees and experience in a specialty area, such as tax, patent, or admiralty law.

Employment growth for lawyers will continue to be concentrated in salaried jobs, as businesses and all levels of government employ a growing number of staff attorneys and as employment in the legal services industry grows in larger law firms. Most salaried positions are in urban areas where government agencies, law firms, and big corporations are concentrated. The number of self-employed lawyers is expected to increase slowly, reflecting the difficulty of establishing a profitable new practice in the face of competition from larger, established law firms. Also, the growing complexity of law, which encourages specialization, and the cost of maintaining up-to-date legal research materials favor larger firms.

For lawyers who wish to work independently, establishing a new practice will probably be easiest in small towns and expanding suburban areas that have an active market for legal services. In such communities, competition from larger, established law firms is likely to be less than in big cities, and new lawyers may find it easier to become known to potential clients.

Some lawyers are adversely affected by cyclical swings in the economy. During recessions, the demand declines for some discretionary legal services, such as planning estates, drafting wills, and handling real estate transactions. Also, corporations are less likely to litigate cases when declining sales and profits result in budgetary restrictions. Some corporations and law firms will not hire new attorneys until business improves or may cut staff to contain costs. Several factors, however, mitigate the overall impact of recessions on lawyers. During recessions, individuals and corporations face other problems requiring legal action, such as bankruptcy, foreclosure, and divorce.

JUDGES

The employment of judges is expected to grow more slowly than the average for all occupations. Contradictory social forces affect the demand for judges. Growing public concerns about crime, safety, and efficient administration of justice should spur demand; on the other hand, tight public funding should slow job growth.

Competition for judgeships will remain keen. Most job openings will arise as judges retire. Traditionally, many judges have held their positions until late in life. Now, early retirement is becoming more common, creating more job openings. However, becoming a judge will still be difficult. Besides competing with other qualified people, judicial candidates must gain political support to be elected or appointed.

Earnings

In 1998, the median annual earnings of all lawyers was $78,170. The middle half of the occupation earned between $51,450 and $114,520. The bottom 10% earned less than $37,310. Median annual earnings in the industries employing the largest numbers of lawyers in 1997 are shown below.

Legal services	$78,700
Federal government	78,200
Fire, marine, and casualty insurance	74,400
State government	59,400
Local government	49,200

Median salaries of lawyers six months after graduation from law school in 1998 varied by type of work, as indicated by Table 4–1.

Salaries of experienced attorneys vary widely according to the type, size, and location of their employer. Lawyers who own their own practices usually earn less than those who are partners in law firms. Lawyers starting their own practice may need to work part-time in other occupations to supplement their income until their practice is well established.

Earnings among judicial workers also vary significantly. According to the Administrative Office of the U.S. Courts, the

TABLE 4–1

Median salaries of lawyers six months after graduation, 1998

Type of Work	*Salary*
All graduates	$45,000
Private practice	60,000
Business/industry	50,000
Academe	38,000
Judicial clerkship	37,500
Government	36,000
Public interest	31,000

Source: National Association for Law Placement

Chief Justice of the U.S. Supreme Court earned $175,400, and the Associate Justices earned $167,900. Federal district court judges had salaries of $136,700 in 1998, as did judges in the Court of Federal Claims and the Court of International Trade; circuit court judges earned $145,000 a year. Federal judges with limited jurisdiction, such as magistrates and bankruptcy court judges, had salaries of $125,800.

According to a survey by the National Center for State Courts, the annual salaries of associate justices of the highest state courts averaged $105,100 in 1997 and ranged from about $77,100 to $137,300. Salaries of state intermediate appellate court judges averaged $103,700 and ranged from $79,400 to $124,200. Salaries of state judges of general jurisdiction trial courts averaged $94,000 and ranged from $72,000 to $115,300.

Most salaried lawyers and judges are provided health and life insurance, and contributions are made on their behalf to retirement plans. Lawyers who practice independently are only covered if they arrange and pay for such benefits themselves.

Related Occupations

Legal training is useful in many other occupations. Some of these are arbitrator, mediator, journalist, patent agent, title examiner, legislative assistant, lobbyist, FBI special agent, political officeholder, and corporate executive.

$\mathcal{S}$ources of Additional Information

Information on law schools and a career in law can be obtained from

American Bar Association
750 North Lake Shore Dr.
Chicago, IL 60611
Internet: http://www.abanet.org

For information on the LSAT, the Law School Data Assembly Service, applying to law school, and financial aid for law students, contact

Law School Admission Council
P.O. Box 40
Newtown, PA 18940
Internet: http://www.lsac.org

Information on acquiring a job as a lawyer with the federal government can be obtained from the Office of Personnel Management through a telephone-based system. Consult your telephone directory under "U.S. Government" for a local number, or call (912) 757-3000; TDD (912) 744-2299. These numbers are not toll free, and charges may result. Information also is available from the Office of Personnel Management's Internet site: http://www.usajobs.opm.gov.

The requirements for admission to the bar in a particular state or other jurisdiction can be obtained at the state capital from the clerk of the state supreme court or the administrator of the state board of bar examiners.

CHAPTER 5

Working as a Correctional Officer

Significant Points

- The work of a correctional officer can be stressful because of concern for personal safety.
- Job opportunities are expected to be very favorable due to much faster than average employment growth coupled with high turnover.
- Most jobs are in large regional jails or in prisons in rural areas.

Nature of the Work

Correctional officers are responsible for overseeing individuals who have been arrested, who are awaiting trial or other

The material in this chapter is adapted from Bureau of Labor Statistics, U.S. Department of Labor, *Occupational Outlook Handbook*, 2000-01 Edition, Bulletin 2520. Superintendent of Documents, U.S. Government Printing Office, Washington, D.C., 2000.

hearing, or who have been convicted of a crime and sentenced to serve time in a jail, reformatory, or penitentiary. Correctional officers maintain security and observe inmate conduct and behavior to prevent disturbances and escapes.

Correctional officers' duties vary with the setting in which they are performed. The majority of the approximately 3,300 jails in the United States are operated by county governments, with about three-quarters of all jails under the jurisdiction of an elected sheriff. Duty in jails differs from that in prisons in a number of important ways. For instance, the jail population changes constantly. The American jail system processes more than 22 million people a year, with about half a million inmates in jail at any given time. Approximately one million inmates are incarcerated in federal and state prisons. The prison population is far more stable than the jail population.

Many correctional officers are employed by police and sheriffs' departments in county and municipal jails or precinct station houses. These officers often have no law enforcement responsibilities outside the jail. (See Chapter 9, "Working as a Law Enforcement Officer.") Others are employed by large regional jails or state and federal prisons where job duties are specialized. A relatively small number supervise aliens being held by the Immigration and Naturalization Service before being released or deported. Regardless of the setting, correctional officers maintain order within the institution, enforce rules and regulations, and may supplement whatever counseling inmates receive.

To make sure inmates are orderly and obey rules, correctional officers monitor inmates' activities, including working, exercising, eating, and showering. They assign and supervise inmates' work assignments. Sometimes it is necessary for them to search inmates and their living quarters for weapons or drugs, to settle disputes between inmates, and to enforce discipline. Correctional officers cannot show favoritism and must report any inmate who violates the rules. A few officers in prison settings hold security positions in towers, where they are equipped with high-powered rifles. In both jail and prison facilities with direct-supervision cell blocks, officers are unarmed—they are locked in a cell block alone, or with another officer, among the 50 to 100 inmates who reside there. The officers enforce regulations primarily through their interpersonal communications skills, although they can have inmates who do not obey their orders transferred to facilities with less desirable living arrangements and fewer privileges.

Correctional officers periodically inspect the facilities. They may, for example, check cells and other areas of the institution for unsanitary conditions, weapons, drugs, fire hazards, and any evidence of infractions of rules. In addition, they routinely inspect locks, window bars, grille doors, and gates for signs of tampering.

Correctional officers report orally and in writing on inmate conduct and on the quality and quantity of work done by inmates. Officers also report disturbances, violations of rules, and any unusual occurrences. They usually keep a daily record of their activities. In the highest security facilities where the most dangerous inmates are housed, correctional officers can monitor the activities of prisoners from a centralized control center with the aid of closed-circuit television cameras and a computer tracking system. In such an environment, the inmates may not see anyone but officers for days or weeks at a time and only rarely leave their cells.

Depending on the offenders' security classification within the institution, correctional officers may have to escort inmates to and from cells and other areas and accompany them to see authorized visitors. Officers may also escort prisoners between the institution and courtrooms, medical facilities, and other destinations. Officers inspect mail and visitors for prohibited items. Should the need arise, they assist outside law enforcement authorities by helping to investigate crimes committed within their institution or by helping search for escaped inmates.

Correctional sergeants directly supervise correctional officers. They are usually responsible for maintaining security and for directing the activities of a group of inmates during an assigned shift or in an assigned area.

Working Conditions

Correctional officers may work indoors or outdoors, depending on their specific duties. Some correctional institutions are well lit, temperature controlled, and ventilated, but many others are overcrowded, hot, and noisy. Outdoors, weather conditions may be disagreeable, for example when standing watch on a guard tower in cold weather. Working in a correctional institution can be stressful and hazardous; correctional officers are occasionally injured in confrontations with inmates who may feel that they have little to lose from violent behavior.

Correctional officers usually work an eight-hour day, five days a week, on rotating shifts. Prison and jail security must be provided around the clock, which often means that junior officers work weekends, holidays, and nights. In addition, officers may be required to work paid overtime.

Employment

Correctional officers held about 383,000 jobs in 1998. Six of every ten worked at state correctional institutions such as prisons, prison camps, and reformatories. Most of the remainder worked at city and county jails or other institutions run by local governments. About 12,000 correctional officers worked at federal correctional institutions, and about 10,400 worked in privately owned and managed prisons.

Most correctional officers work in relatively large institutions located in rural areas, although a significant number work in jails and other smaller facilities located in law enforcement agencies throughout the country.

Training, Other Qualifications, and Advancement

Most institutions require that correctional officers be at least 18 or 21 years of age, have a high school education or its equivalent, have no felony convictions, and be a U.S. citizen. In addition, correctional institutions increasingly seek correctional officers with postsecondary education, particularly in psychology, criminal justice, police science, criminology, and related fields.

Correctional officers must be in good health. The federal system and many states require candidates to meet formal standards of physical fitness, eyesight, and hearing. Strength, good judgment, and the ability to think and act quickly are indispensable. The federal system and some states screen applicants for drug abuse, require candidates to pass a written or oral examination, and conduct a background check.

Federal, state, and some local departments of corrections provide training for correctional officers based on guidelines established by the American Correctional Association, the American Jail Association, and other professional organizations. Some states have regional training academies for the use of local agencies. All states and local departments of correction provide on-the-job training at the conclusion of formal instruction. Officer trainees receive several weeks or months of training in the actual job setting under the supervision of an experienced officer. Entry requirements and on-the-job training vary widely from agency to agency.

Academy trainees generally receive instruction on institutional policies, regulations, and operations, as well as custody and security procedures, among other subjects. New federal correctional officers must undergo 200 hours of formal training within the first year of employment. They must complete 120 hours of specialized correctional instruction at the federal Bureau of Prisons residential training center at Glynco, Georgia, within the first 60 days after appointment. Experienced officers receive in-service training to keep abreast of new ideas and procedures.

Some correctional officers have the opportunity to join prison tactical response teams, which are trained to respond to riots, hostage situations, forced cell moves, and other potentially dangerous confrontations. Team members often receive monthly training and practice with weapons, chemical agents, forced entry methods, and other tactics.

With education, experience, and training, qualified officers may advance to correctional sergeant or other supervisory or administrative positions. Many correctional institutions require experience as a correctional officer for other corrections positions. Ambitious correctional officers can be promoted all the way up to warden. Officers sometimes transfer to related occupations, such as parole officer.

*J*ob Outlook

Job opportunities for correctional officers are expected to be very favorable through 2008. The need to replace correctional officers who transfer to other occupations or who leave the labor force, coupled with rising employment demand, will generate many thousands of job openings each year. In addition, some local and a few state correctional agencies have traditionally experienced difficulty in attracting qualified applicants, largely due to relatively low salaries and the concentration of jobs in rural locations. This situation is expected to continue.

Employment of correctional officers is expected to increase faster than the average for all occupations through the year 2008 as additional officers are hired to supervise and control the growing inmate population. Increasing public concern about the spread of crime and illegal drugs—resulting in more arrests and more convictions—and the adoption of mandatory sentencing guidelines calling for longer sentences and reduced parole for inmates will spur demand for correctional officers. Expansion and new construction of correctional facilities also are expected to create many new jobs for correctional officers, although state and local government budgetary constraints could affect the rate at which new facilities are built and staffed. Some employment opportunities also may arise in the private sector as public authorities opt to contract with private companies to provide and staff correctional facilities.

Layoffs of correctional officers are rare because security must be maintained in correctional institutions at all times.

*E*arnings

Median annual earnings of correctional officers were $28,540 in 1998. The middle 50% earned between $22,930 and $37,550. The lowest 10% had earnings of less than $18,810, while the top 10% earned over $46,320. Median annual earnings in the industries employing the largest numbers of correctional officers in 1997 in the public sector were $32,600 in the federal government, $29,700 in local government, and $27,300 in state government. In the management and public relations industry, where officers employed by privately operated prisons are classified, median annual earnings were $18,500.

According to a 1999 survey in *Corrections Compendium*, a national journal for corrections professionals, there is no common pattern or trend in correctional salaries around the United States. The variance between the low and high starting salaries exists for all positions and for personnel of all experience levels. Beginning salaries for state correctional officers ranged from $14,600 in California to $34,100 in New Jersey. The median salary for correctional officers with more than one year of experience ranged from $18,000 in Mississippi to $44,800 in New Jersey.

At the federal level, the starting salary was about $20,600 to $23,000 a year in 1999; supervisory correctional officers started at about $28,200 a year. Starting salaries were slightly higher in selected areas where prevailing local pay levels were higher. The annual average salary for correctional officers employed by the federal government was $36,500 in early 1999.

Correctional officers employed in the public sector are usually given uniforms or a clothing allowance to purchase their own uniforms. Most are provided or can participate in hospitalization or major medical insurance plans; many officers can get disability and life insurance at group rates. They also receive vacation and sick leave and pension benefits. Officers employed by the federal government and most state governments are covered by civil service systems or merit boards. Their retirement coverage entitles them to retire at age 50 after 20 years of service or at any age with 25 years of service. In the federal system and in some states, many correctional officers are represented by labor unions.

Related Occupations

A number of related careers are open to high school graduates who are interested in protective services and the field of security. Bodyguards escort people and protect them from injury or invasion of privacy. House or store detectives patrol business establishments to protect against theft and vandalism and to enforce standards of good behavior. Security guards protect government, commercial, and industrial property against theft, vandalism, illegal entry, and fire. Police officers and deputy sheriffs maintain law and order, prevent crime, and arrest offenders. Probation and parole officers monitor and counsel offenders and evaluate their progress in becoming productive members of society.

Sources of Additional Information

Information about correctional jobs in jails is available from

American Jail Association
2053 Day Rd., Suite 100
Hagerstown, MD 21740
Internet: http://www.corrections.com/aja/index.html

For information about careers as a correctional officer in jails and prisons, contact

International Association of Correctional Officers (IACO)
P.O. Box 81826
Lincoln, NE 68501

Information on entrance requirements, training, and career opportunities for federal correctional officers may be obtained by calling the Federal Bureau of Prisons at (800) 347-7744 or by visiting http://www.bop.gov.

Information on obtaining a job with the federal government is available from the Office of Personnel Management through a telephone-based system. Consult your telephone directory under "U.S. Government" for a local number, or call (912) 757-3000; TDD (912) 744-2299. These numbers are not toll free, and charges may result. Information is also available from the Office of Personnel Management's Internet site: http://www.usajobs.opm.gov.

CHAPTER 6

Working as a Firefighter

Significant Points

- Fire fighting involves hazardous conditions and long, irregular hours.
- Keen competition for jobs is expected. Many people are attracted to the occupation because it provides considerable job security and the opportunity to perform an essential public service.

Nature of the Work

Firefighters respond to a variety of emergency situations in which life, property, or the environment is at risk. They are

The material in this chapter is adapted from Bureau of Labor Statistics, U.S. Department of Labor, *Occupational Outlook Handbook*, 2000-01 Edition, Bulletin 2520. Superintendent of Documents, U.S. Government Printing Office, Washington, D.C., 2000.

frequently the first emergency response team at the scene of an accident, fire, flood, earthquake, or act of terrorism. Every year, fires and other emergency conditions take thousands of lives and destroy property worth billions of dollars. Firefighters help protect the public against these dangers. This chapter provides information about career firefighters only; it does not cover volunteer firefighters, who perform the same duties and sometimes comprise the majority of firefighters in a residential area.

Most calls to which firefighters respond involve medical emergencies, and many fire departments provide ambulance service for victims. Firefighters receive training in emergency medical procedures, and many fire departments require personnel to be certified as emergency medical technicians.

During duty hours, firefighters must be prepared to respond immediately to a fire or any other emergency situation that arises. Each situation a firefighter encounters is unique. Because firefighting is dangerous and complex, it requires organization and teamwork. At every emergency scene, firefighters perform specific duties assigned by a superior officer. They may connect hose lines to hydrants, operate a pump or other equipment, or position ladders. They may rescue victims and administer emergency medical aid, ventilate smoke-filled areas, and salvage the contents of buildings. Their duties may change several times while the company is in action. Sometimes firefighters remain at the site of a disaster for several days or more, rescuing survivors and assisting with medical emergencies.

The job of firefighter has become more complicated in recent years due to the use of increasingly sophisticated equipment and the need to assume a wider range of responsibilities. These responsibilities include emergency medical treatment, assisting in the recovery from natural disasters such as earthquakes and tornadoes, and the control, prevention, and cleanup of oil spills and incidents involving other hazardous materials.

Most firefighters are primarily involved with protecting business and residential structures, but some work at airports on crash and rescue crews, at chemical plants, by waterfronts, and in forests and wilderness areas. In forests, air patrols locate fires and report their findings to headquarters by telephone or radio. Fire rangers patrol areas of the forest to locate and report fires and hazardous conditions and to ensure that travelers and campers comply with fire regulations. When fires break out, firefighters use hand tools and water hoses to battle the blaze. Some specialized firefighters parachute from airplanes when necessary to reach inaccessible areas.

Most fire departments have a fire-prevention division, usually headed by a fire marshal. Fire inspectors conduct inspections of structures to prevent fires and to ensure compliance with the fire code. These firefighters may also work with developers and planners to check and approve plans for new buildings. Fire-prevention personnel often speak on these subjects before public assemblies and civic organizations. Some firefighters become fire investigators, who determine the origin and causes of fires. They collect evidence, interview witnesses, and prepare reports on fires in cases where the cause may be arson or criminal negligence. Some investigators have police powers and may arrest suspects. They may also be called upon to testify in court.

Between alarms, firefighters participate in educational activities. In addition to taking classes themselves, they sometimes give lectures or demonstrations on safety issues to the local community. They may also clean and maintain equipment, conduct practice drills and fire inspections, and participate in physical fitness activities. They prepare written reports on fire incidents and review fire science literature to keep abreast of technological developments and changing administrative practices and policies.

Working Conditions

Firefighters spend much of their time at fire stations, which usually have features common to a residential facility. When an alarm comes in, firefighters must respond rapidly, regardless of the weather or the hour. They may spend long periods on their feet, sometimes in adverse weather, tending to fires, medical emergencies, incidents involving hazardous materials, and other emergencies.

Firefighting is a very hazardous occupation. It involves risk of death or injury from sudden cave-ins of floors or toppling walls and from exposure to flames and smoke. Strong winds and falling trees and branches can make fighting forest fires particularly dangerous. Firefighters may also come in contact with poisonous, flammable, or explosive gases and chemicals or radioactive or other hazardous materials that could have immediate or long-term effects on their health. For these reasons, they must wear appropriate protective gear, which can be very heavy.

Work hours of firefighters are longer and vary more widely than hours of most other workers. Many work more than 50 hours a week. During some weeks, they may work significantly longer hours. In some cities, they are on duty for 24 hours, then off for 48 hours, and receive an extra day off at intervals. In other cities, they work a day shift of 10 hours for three or four days, a night shift of 14 hours for three or four nights, have three or four days off, and then repeat the cycle. In addition, firefighters often work extra hours at fires and other emergencies and are regularly assigned to work on holidays. Fire lieutenants and fire captains often work the same hours as the firefighters they supervise. Duty hours include time when firefighters study, train, and perform fire-prevention duties.

*E*mployment

Paid firefighters held about 314,000 jobs in 1998. More than nine of every 10 worked in municipal or county fire departments. Some very large cities have several thousand firefighters, while many small towns have only a few. Most of the remaining10% of firefighters in 1998 worked in fire departments on federal and state installations, including airports. Private fire-fighting companies employed a small number of firefighters.

In response to the expanding role of firefighters, some municipalities have combined fire prevention, public fire education, safety, and emergency medical services into a single public safety organization. Some local and regional fire departments are being consolidated into countywide establishments to cut overhead, take advantage of economies of scale, reduce administrative staffs, and establish consistent training standards and work procedures.

Training, Other Qualifications, and Advancement

Applicants for municipal fire-fighting jobs may have to pass a written test; tests of strength, physical stamina, coordination, and agility; and a medical examination, including a drug screening. Workers also may be monitored on a random basis for drug use after accepting employment. Examinations are generally open to applicants who are at least 18 years of age and have a high school diploma or the equivalent. Those who receive the highest scores in all phases of testing have the best chances for appointment. The completion of community college courses in fire science may improve an applicant's chances for appointment. In recent years, an increasing proportion of entrants to this occupation have had some postsecondary education.

As a rule, beginners in large fire departments are trained for several weeks at the department's training center. Through classroom instruction and practical training, the recruits study fire-fighting techniques, fire prevention, hazardous materials, local building codes, and emergency medical procedures, including first aid and cardiopulmonary resuscitation. They also learn how to use axes, saws, fire extinguishers, ladders, and other fire-fighting and rescue equipment. After successfully completing this training, they are assigned to a fire company, where they undergo a period of probation.

A number of fire departments have accredited apprenticeship programs lasting up to five years. These programs combine formal technical instruction with on-the-job training under the supervision of experienced firefighters. Technical instruction covers subjects such as fire-fighting techniques and equipment, chemical hazards associated with various combustible building materials, emergency medical procedures, and fire prevention and safety.

Most experienced firefighters continue studying to improve their job performance and to prepare for promotion examinations. Today, firefighters need more training to operate increasingly sophisticated equipment and to deal safely with the greater hazards associated with fighting fires in larger, more complex structures. To progress to higher-level positions, they must acquire expertise in the most advanced fire-fighting equipment and techniques and in building construction, emergency medical technology, writing, public speaking, management and budgeting procedures, and labor relations. Fire departments frequently conduct training programs, and some firefighters attend training sessions sponsored by the National Fire Academy. These training sessions cover various topics, including executive development, anti-arson techniques, disaster preparedness, hazardous materials control, and public fire safety and education. Some states also have extensive firefighter training and certification programs.

Many colleges and universities offer courses leading to two- or four-year degrees in fire engineering or fire science. Many fire departments offer firefighters incentives such as tuition reimbursement or higher pay for completing advanced training.

Among the personal qualities firefighters need are mental alertness, self-discipline, courage, mechanical aptitude, endurance, strength, and a sense of public service. Initiative and good judgment are extremely important because firefighters independently make quick decisions in emergencies. Because members of a crew live and work closely together under conditions of stress and danger for extended periods, they should be dependable and able to get along well with others in a group. Leadership qualities are necessary for officers, who must establish and maintain discipline and efficiency and direct the activities of firefighters in their companies.

Opportunities for promotion are good in most fire departments. As firefighters gain expertise, they may advance to a higher rank. The line of promotion is usually to engineer, lieutenant, captain, battalion chief, assistant chief, deputy chief, and finally chief. Advancement is generally based on scores on a written examination, job performance, interviews, and seniority. Increasingly, fire departments are using assessment centers—which simulate a variety of actual job performance tasks—to screen for the best candidates for promotion. Many fire departments now require a bachelor's degree, preferably in fire science, public administration, or a related field, for promotion to positions higher than battalion chief. Some departments also require a master's degree for the chief. A master's degree is also required for executive fire officer certification from the National Fire Academy and for state chief officer certification.

Job Outlook

Prospective firefighters are expected to face keen competition for available job openings. Firefighting attracts many people because a high school education is usually sufficient, earnings are relatively high, and a pension is guaranteed upon retirement. In addition, the work is frequently exciting and challenging and affords an opportunity to perform a valuable public service. Consequently, the number of qualified applicants in most areas generally exceeds the number of job openings, even though the written examination and physical requirements eliminate many applicants. This situation is expected to persist in coming years.

The employment of firefighters is expected to increase more slowly than the average for all occupations through the year 2008, as fire departments continue to compete with other public service providers for funding. Most growth in employment will be due to an expected increase in the number of positions for paid firefighters versus volunteer fire-fighters because the increased level of specialized training required in this occupation makes it more difficult for volunteer firefighters to remain qualified. Little employment growth is expected in large, urban fire departments. A small number of local governments are expected to contract with private companies for fire-fighting services.

The turnover of firefighter jobs is unusually low, particularly for a hazardous occupation that requires a relatively limited investment in formal education. Nevertheless, many job openings are expected to result from the need to replace those who retire, stop working for other reasons, or transfer to other occupations.

Layoffs of firefighters are uncommon. Fire protection is an essential service, and citizens are likely to exert considerable pressure on city officials to expand or at least preserve the level of fire-protection coverage. Even when budget cuts do occur, local fire departments usually cut expenses by postponing equipment purchases or by not hiring new firefighters rather than by laying off staff.

Earnings

Median annual earnings of firefighters were $31,170 in 1998. The middle 50% earned between $22,370 and $40,840. The lowest 10% earned less than $14,310, and the highest 10% earned more than $50,930. Firefighters employed in local government, except education and hospitals, had median earnings of $31,400 in 1997; those employed by state government, except in schools and hospitals, had median earnings of $29,400; and firefighters in the federal government had median earnings of $26,900.

Median annual earnings of fire-fighting and fire-prevention supervisors were $44,830 in 1998. The middle 50% earned between $34,020 and $59,610. The lowest 10% earned less than $23,050, and the highest 10% earned more than $81,570. Fire-fighting and fire-prevention supervisors employed in local government, except in schools and hospitals, earned about $45,200 in 1997. Median annual earnings of fire-inspection occupations were $40,040 in 1998. The middle 50% earned between $30,500 and $50,610. The lowest 10% earned less than $22,150, and the highest 10% earned more than $73,570.

The International City-County Management Association's annual Police and Fire Personnel, Salaries, and Expenditures Survey revealed that 89% of the municipalities surveyed provided fire-protection services in 1997. The following 1997 salaries pertain to sworn full-time positions.

Firefighter	$26,900–35,200
Engineer	32,200–39,800
Fire lieutenant	35,100–41,100
Fire captain	37,500–44,700
Assistant fire chief	43,900–53,200
Battalion chief	45,300–56,000
Deputy chief	45,900–56,900
Fire chief	52,700–66,000

Firefighters who average more than a certain number of hours a week must be paid overtime. The department determines the hours threshold during the firefighter's work period, which ranges from seven to 28 days. Firefighters often earn overtime for working extra shifts to maintain minimum staffing levels or for special emergencies.

The benefits firefighters receive usually include medical and liability insurance, vacation and sick leave, and some paid holidays. Almost all fire departments provide protective clothing (helmets, boots, and coats) and breathing apparatus, and many also provide dress uniforms. Firefighters are generally covered by pension plans, often providing retirement at half pay after 25 years of service or if disabled in the line of duty.

Many career firefighters are represented by the International Association of Firefighters, and many chief officers belong to the International Association of Fire Chiefs.

Related Occupations

An occupation closely related to fire protection is fire-protection engineer, in which the engineer identifies fire hazards in homes and workplaces and designs prevention programs and automatic fire-detection and extinguishing systems. Other occupations in which workers respond to emergencies include police officer and emergency medical technician.

Sources of Additional Information

Information about a career as a firefighter can be obtained from local fire departments and from the following organizations:

International Association of Firefighters
1750 New York Ave. N.W.
Washington, DC 20006
Internet: http://www.iaff.org/iaff/index.html

U.S. Fire Administration
16825 South Seton Ave.
Emmitsburg, MD 21727

Information about professional qualifications for firefighters and a list of colleges and universities offering two- or four-year degree programs in fire science or fire prevention is available from

National Fire Academy
Degrees at a Distance Program
16825 South Seton Ave.
Emmitsburg, MD 21727
Internet: http://www.usfa.fema.gov/nfa/index.htm

CHAPTER 7

Working as an Inspector or Compliance Officer

Significant Points

- About four out of every five inspection and compliance jobs are in federal, state, and local government agencies that enforce rules on health, safety, food quality, licensing, and finance.
- Because of the diversity of the functions they perform, qualifications for inspector and compliance officer jobs vary widely.

Nature of the Work

Inspectors and compliance officers enforce a wide range of laws, regulations, policies, and procedures. They inspect and

The material in this chapter is adapted from Bureau of Labor Statistics, U.S. Department of Labor, *Occupational Outlook Handbook*, 2000-01 Edition, Bulletin 2520. Superintendent of Documents, U.S. Government Printing Office, Washington, D.C., 2000.

enforce rules on matters such as health, safety, food, licensing, and finance. Inspectors' and compliance officers' duties vary widely.

Agricultural commodity graders apply quality standards to aid the buying and selling of commodities and to ensure that retailers and consumers know the quality of the products they purchase. Although this grading is not required by law, buyers may not be willing to purchase ungraded commodities. Graders usually specialize in a particular type of agricultural product, such as eggs, meat, poultry, processed or fresh fruits and vegetables, grain, tobacco, cotton, and dairy products. They examine product samples to determine quality and grade, and they issue official grading certificates. To maintain sanitation standards, graders may inspect the plant and equipment used in processing.

Attendance officers investigate continued absences of pupils from public schools.

Aviation safety inspectors ensure that Federal Aviation Administration (FAA) regulations that govern the quality, performance, and safety of aircraft equipment, operations, and personnel are followed. Aviation safety inspectors may inspect aircraft and equipment manufacturing, maintenance, and repair or flight procedures. They may work in the areas of flight operations, maintenance, or avionics, and they usually specialize in either commercial or general aviation aircraft. They also examine and certify aircraft pilots, pilot examiners, flight instructors, repair stations, schools, and instructional materials.

Bank examiners investigate financial institutions to enforce federal or state laws and regulations governing the institution's operations and solvency. Examiners schedule audits, determine actions protecting the institution's solvency and the interests of shareholders and depositors, and recommend acceptance or rejection of applications for merger, acquisition, or establishment of a new institution.

Consumer safety inspectors and *officers* inspect food, feeds, pesticides, weights and measures, biological products, cosmetics, drugs, medical equipment, and radiation-emitting products. Some are proficient in several areas. Working individually or in teams under a senior inspector, they check on firms that produce, handle, store, or market the products they regulate. They ensure that standards are maintained, and they respond to consumer complaints by questioning employees, vendors, and others to obtain evidence. Inspectors look for inaccurate product labeling and for decomposition or chemical or bacterial contamination that could result in a product becoming harmful to health. They may use portable scales, cameras, ultraviolet lights, thermometers, chemical testing kits, radiation monitors, or other equipment to find violations. They may send product samples, collected as part of their examinations, to laboratories for analysis.

After completing their inspection, inspectors discuss their observations with plant managers or officials and point out areas where corrective measures are needed. They write reports of their findings and, when necessary, compile evidence for use in court if legal action must be taken.

Customs inspectors enforce laws governing imports and exports. Stationed in the United States and overseas at airports, seaports, and border crossing points, they examine, count, weigh, gauge, measure, and sample commercial and noncommercial cargoes entering and leaving the United States to determine admissibility and the amount of duty that must be paid. They ensure that all cargo is properly described on accompanying importers' declarations to determine the proper duty and to interdict contraband. They inspect baggage and articles carried by passengers and crew members to ensure that all merchandise is declared, that proper duties are paid, and that contraband is not present. They also ensure that people, ships, planes, and anything used to import or export cargo comply with all appropriate entrance and clearance requirements.

Dealer compliance representatives inspect franchised establishments, such as motels and fast-food restaurants, to ensure compliance with the franchiser's policies and procedures. They may suggest changes in financial or other operations which, if not followed, could result in loss of the franchise.

Environmental health inspectors, who work primarily for state and local governments, ensure that food, water, and air meet government standards. They check the cleanliness and safety of food and beverages produced in dairies and processing plants or served in restaurants, hospitals, and other institutions. They often examine the handling, processing, and serving of food for compliance with sanitation rules and regulations, and they oversee the treatment and disposal of sewage, refuse, and garbage. In addition, inspectors may visit pollution sources and test for pollutants by collecting air, water, or waste samples for analysis. They try to determine the nature and cause of pollution and initiate action to stop it.

In large local and state health or agriculture departments, environmental health inspectors may specialize in a particular area, such as milk and dairy products, food sanitation, waste control, air pollution, water pollution, institutional sanitation, or occupational health. In rural areas and small towns, they may be responsible for a wide range of environmental health activities.

Equal opportunity representatives ascertain and correct unfair employment practices through consultation with and mediation between employers and minority groups.

Federal and state laws require *food inspectors* to inspect meat, poultry, their byproducts, and egg products to ensure that they are safe for public consumption. Working on-site, frequently as part of a team, they inspect meat and poultry slaughtering, processing, and packaging operations, as well as egg products operations. They also check for correct product labeling and proper sanitation.

Immigration inspectors interview and examine people seeking entrance to the United States and its territories. They inspect passports to determine whether people are legally eligible to enter, and they verify their citizenship status and identity. Immigration inspectors also prepare reports, maintain records, and process applications and petitions for immigration or temporary residence in the United States.

Logging operations inspectors review contract logging operations. They prepare reports and issue remedial instructions for violations of contractual agreements and of fire and safety regulations.

Mine safety and health inspectors work to ensure the health and safety of miners. They visit mines and related facilities to obtain information on health and safety conditions and to enforce safety laws and regulations. They discuss their findings with the management of the mine, and they issue citations describing violations and hazards that must be corrected. Mine inspectors also investigate and report on mine accidents and may direct rescue and fire-fighting operations when fires or explosions occur.

Motor vehicle inspectors verify the compliance of automobiles and trucks with state requirements for safe operation and emissions. They inspect truck cargoes to ensure compliance with legal limitations on gross weight and hazardous cargoes.

Occupational safety and health inspectors visit places of employment to detect unsafe machinery and equipment or unhealthy working conditions. They discuss their findings with the employer or plant manager and order that violations be promptly corrected in accordance with federal, state, or local government safety standards and regulations. They interview supervisors and employees in response to complaints or accidents, and they may order suspension of activity posing a threat to workers.

Park rangers enforce laws and regulations in state and national parks. Their duties range from registering vehicles and visitors, collecting fees, and providing information regarding park use and points of interest, to patrolling areas to prevent fire, participating in first aid and rescue activities, and training and supervising other park workers. Some rangers specialize in snow safety and avalanche control. With increasing numbers of visitors to our national parks, some rangers function as law enforcement officers.

Postal inspectors observe the functioning of the postal system and enforce laws and regulations. As law enforcement agents, postal inspectors have statutory powers of arrest and the authority to carry firearms. They investigate criminal activities, such as theft and misuse of the mail. In instances of suspected mismanagement or fraud, inspectors conduct management or financial audits. They also collaborate with other government agencies, such as the Internal Revenue Service, as members of special task forces.

Railroad inspectors verify the compliance of railroad systems and equipment with federal safety regulations. They investigate accidents and review railroads' operating practices.

Revenue officers investigate and collect delinquent tax returns from individuals or businesses. They investigate leads from various sources. They attempt to resolve tax problems with taxpayers, and they recommend penalties, collection actions, and criminal prosecutions when necessary.

Securities compliance examiners implement regulations concerning securities and real estate transactions. They investigate applications for registration of securities sales and complaints of irregular securities transactions, and they recommend legal action when necessary.

Travel accommodations raters inspect hotels, motels, restaurants, campgrounds, and vacation resorts. They evaluate travel and tourist accommodations for travel guide publishers, tourism promoters, automobile clubs, and other organizations.

Other inspectors and compliance officers include coroners, code inspectors, and mortician investigators. Closely related work is done by construction and building inspectors.

Working Conditions

Inspectors and compliance officers meet all kinds of people and work in a variety of environments. Their jobs often involve considerable fieldwork, and some inspectors travel frequently. They are generally furnished with a vehicle or are reimbursed for travel expenses.

Inspectors may experience unpleasant, stressful, and dangerous working conditions. For example, mine safety and health inspectors are exposed to the same hazards as miners. Some food inspectors examine and inspect the operation of slaughterhouses and frequently come in contact with unpleasant conditions. Postal inspectors have to put up with the stress inherent in all law enforcement work, in addition to the danger inherent in making occasional arrests. Park rangers often work outdoors—in many cases, in rugged terrain—in very hot or bitterly cold weather for extended periods.

Many inspectors work long and often irregular hours. Even those inspectors not engaged in some form of law enforcement may find themselves in adversarial roles when the organization or individual being inspected objects to the inspection.

*E*mployment

Inspectors and compliance officers held about 176,000 jobs in 1998. State governments employed 30%, the federal government—chiefly the Departments of Defense, Labor, Treasury, and Agriculture—employed 31%, and local governments employed 19%. The remaining 20% were employed throughout the private sector, primarily in schools, hospitals, insurance companies, labor unions, and manufacturing firms.

Consumer safety inspectors work in a variety of settings. Some work for the U.S. Food and Drug Administration, but the majority of these inspectors work for state governments. Most food inspectors and agricultural commodity graders are employed by the U.S. Department of Agriculture. Many health inspectors work for state and local governments. Compliance inspectors are employed primarily by the Treasury and Labor Departments on the federal level, as well as by state and local governments. The Department of Defense employs the most quality assurance inspectors. The states and the U.S. Treasury Department employ internal revenue officers. Aviation safety inspectors work for the Federal Aviation Administration. The Environmental Protection Agency employs inspectors to verify compliance with pollution control and other laws. The U.S. Department of Labor and many state governments employ occupational safety and health inspectors, equal opportunity officers, and mine safety and health inspectors. The Department of Interior employs park rangers. Department of Treasury customs inspectors work in the United States and overseas at airports, seaports, and border crossing points.

*T*raining, Other Qualifications, and Advancement

Because of the diversity of the functions they perform, qualifications for inspector and compliance officer jobs differ greatly. Requirements include a combination of education and experience and often a passing grade on a written examination. Employers may require college training, including courses related to the job. The following examples illustrate the range of qualifications for various inspector jobs.

Postal inspector applicants must have a bachelor's degree and one year of work experience. It is desirable that they have one of several professional certifications, such as certified public accountant. They also must pass a background suitability investigation, meet certain health requirements, undergo a drug-screening test, possess a valid state driver's license, and be a U.S. citizen between 21 and 36 years of age when hired.

Aviation safety inspectors working in operations must be pilots with varying certificates, ratings, and numbers of flight hours to their credit. In addition, FAA medical certificates are required. Some aviation inspectors must also have an FAA flight instructor rating. Maintenance and avionics inspectors must have considerable experience in aviation maintenance and knowledge of industry standards and relevant federal laws. Many aviation safety inspectors have had flight and maintenance training in the armed forces. No written examination is required.

Applicants for positions as mine safety and health inspectors generally must have experience in mine safety, management, or supervision. Some positions, such as mine electrical inspector, may require specialized skills. Applicants must meet strict medical requirements and must be physically able to perform arduous duties efficiently. Many mine safety inspectors are former miners.

An applicant for internal revenue officer must be a U.S. citizen and have a bachelor's degree or three years of experience in business, legal, financial, or investigative practices.

Park rangers need at least two years of college with at least 12 credits in science and criminal justice, although some start as part-time, seasonal workers with the U.S. Forest Service. Most positions require a bachelor's degree.

Environmental health inspectors, called "sanitarians" in many states, must sometimes have a bachelor's degree in environmental health or in the physical or biological sciences. In most states, they are licensed by examining boards.

All inspectors and compliance officers are trained in the applicable laws or inspection procedures through some combination of classroom and on-the-job training. In general, people who want to enter this occupation should be responsible and like detailed work. Inspectors and compliance officers should be neat and personable and should be able to communicate well orally and in writing.

Federal government inspectors and compliance officers whose job performance is satisfactory advance up their career ladder to a specified full performance level. For positions above this level (usually supervisory positions), advancement is competitive, based on agency needs and individual merit. Advancement opportunities in state and local governments and in the private sector are often similar to those in the federal government.

Some civil service specifications, including those for mine inspectors, aviation safety inspectors, and agricultural commodity graders, rate applicants solely on their experience and education. Others require a written examination.

*J*ob Outlook

Average growth in employment of inspectors and compliance officers is expected through the year 2008, reflecting a balance of continuing public demand for a safe environment and quality products against the desire for smaller government and fewer regulations. Additional job openings will arise primarily from the need to replace those who transfer to other occupations, retire, or leave the labor force for other reasons. In private industry, employment growth will reflect industry growth, due to continuing self-enforcement of government and company regulations and policies, particularly among franchise operations in various industries.

The employment of inspectors and compliance officers is seldom affected by general economic fluctuations. Federal, state, and local governments—which employ most inspectors—provide workers with considerable job security.

*E*arnings

The median annual salary of inspectors and compliance officers, except construction, was about $36,820 in 1998. The lowest 10% earned less than $22,750; the highest 10% earned over $72,280. In the federal government, the annual starting salaries for inspectors varied from $25,500 to $31,200, depending on the nature of the inspection or compliance activity. Beginning salaries were slightly higher in selected areas where the prevailing local pay level was higher. The following chart presents average salaries for selected inspectors and compliance officers in the federal government in non-supervisory, supervisory, and managerial positions in 1999.

Air safety investigator	$68,900
Highway safety inspector	68,100
Mine safety and health inspector	65,100
Railroad safety inspector	60,500
Internal revenue agent	58,000
Equal employment opportunity official	58,000
Environmental protection specialist	57,900
Safety and occupational health manager	54,000

Import specialist	$49,370
Quality assurance inspector	50,600
Customs inspector	40,020
Securities compliance examiner	43,300
Agricultural commodity grader	41,600
Immigration inspector	35,010
Consumer safety inspector	37,300
Food inspector	35,200
Environmental protection assistant	31,600

Most inspectors and compliance officers work for federal, state, and local governments and in large private firms, all of which generally offer more generous benefits than do smaller firms.

Related Occupations

Inspectors and compliance officers are responsible for seeing that laws and regulations are obeyed. Construction and building inspectors; fire marshals; federal, state, and local law enforcement professionals; correctional officers; and fish and game wardens also enforce laws and regulations.

Sources of Additional Information

Information on obtaining a job with the federal government can be obtained from the Office of Personnel Management through a telephone-based system. Consult your telephone directory under "U.S. Government" for a local number, or call (912) 757-3000; TDD (912) 744-2299. These numbers are not toll free, and charges may result. Information is also available from the Office of Personnel Management's Internet site: http://www.usajobs.opm.gov.

For information on a career as a specific type of federal inspector or compliance officer, contact the federal department or agency that employs them.

Information about state and local government jobs is available from state civil service commissions, which are usually located in state capitals, and from local government offices.

Information about jobs in private industry is available from the state employment service, which is listed in the state government section of local telephone directories under "Job Service" or "Employment."

CHAPTER 8

Working as a Paralegal

Significant Points

- While some paralegals train on the job, employers increasingly prefer to hire graduates of postsecondary paralegal training programs.
- Paralegals are projected to rank among the fastest growing occupation in the economy as they increasingly perform many legal tasks formerly carried out by lawyers.
- Stiff competition is expected as the number of graduates of paralegal training programs and others seeking to enter the profession outpaces job growth.

The material in this chapter is adapted from Bureau of Labor Statistics, U.S. Department of Labor, *Occupational Outlook Handbook*, 2000-01 Edition, Bulletin 2520. Superintendent of Documents, U.S. Government Printing Office, Washington, D.C., 2000.

*N*ature of the Work

Not all legal work requires a law degree. Lawyers are often assisted in their work by paralegals or legal assistants. Paralegals perform many of the same tasks as lawyers, except for those considered to be the practice of law.

Paralegals work for lawyers. Although the lawyers assume responsibility for the legal work, they often delegate many of their tasks to paralegals. Paralegals are prohibited from setting legal fees, giving legal advice, and presenting cases in court.

Paralegals generally do the preparatory work for lawyers involved in closings, hearings, trials, and corporate meetings. Paralegals investigate the facts of a case, ensuring that all relevant information is uncovered. They conduct legal research to identify the appropriate laws, judicial decisions, legal articles, and other materials that are relevant to an assigned case. After organizing and analyzing the information, paralegals may prepare written reports that attorneys use in determining how cases should be handled. Should the attorney decide to file a lawsuit on behalf of the client, the paralegal may help prepare the legal arguments, draft pleadings and motions to be filed with the court, obtain affidavits, and assist attorneys during trials. Paralegals also organize and track files of all documents and correspondence important to cases and make them available to attorneys.

Paralegals may work in all areas of the law, including litigation, bankruptcy, corporate law, criminal law, employee benefits, patent and copyright law, and real estate. They help draft contracts, mortgages, separation agreements, and trust instruments. They may also help prepare tax returns and plan estates. Some paralegals coordinate the activities of other law office employees and keep the financial records for the office.

Paralegals who work for corporations help attorneys with employee contracts, shareholder agreements, stock option plans, and employee benefit plans. They may help prepare and file annual financial reports, maintain corporate minute books and resolutions, and help secure loans for the corporation. Paralegals may also review government regulations to ensure that the corporation operates within the law.

The duties of paralegals who work in government vary depending on the agency in which they are employed. Generally, paralegals in government analyze legal material for internal use, maintain reference files, conduct research for attorneys, collect and analyze evidence for agency hearings, and prepare informative or explanatory material on the law, agency regulations, and agency policy for general use by the agency and the public.

Paralegals employed in community legal service projects help the poor, the aged, and others in need of legal assistance. They file forms, conduct research, and prepare documents. When authorized by law, they may represent clients at administrative hearings.

Some paralegals, usually those in small and medium-sized law firms, perform a variety of duties that require a general knowledge of the law. For example, they may research judicial decisions on improper police arrests or help prepare a mortgage contract.

Some paralegals employed by large law firms, government agencies, and corporations specialize in one aspect of the law, including real estate, estate planning, family law, labor law, litigation, and corporate law. Within these specialties, functions are often broken down further, so paralegals may deal with a specific area. For example, paralegals specializing in labor law may deal exclusively with employee benefits.

A growing number of paralegals use computers in their work. Computer software packages and online legal research are increasingly used to search legal literature stored in computer databases and on CD-ROMs. The Internet is also used extensively for legal research. In litigation involving many supporting documents, paralegals may use computer databases to organize, index, and retrieve the material. Imaging software allows paralegals to scan documents directly into a database. Paralegals sometimes use billing programs to track hours billed to clients. They may also use computer software packages to perform tax computations and to explore the consequences of possible tax strategies for clients.

*W*orking Conditions

Paralegals do most of their work at desks in offices and law libraries. Occasionally, they travel to gather information and to perform other duties.

Paralegals employed by corporations and government usually work a standard 40-hour week. Although most paralegals work year-round, some are temporarily employed during busy times of the year, then released when the workload diminishes. Paralegals who work for law firms sometimes work very long hours when they are under pressure to meet deadlines. Some law firms reward such loyalty with bonuses and additional time off.

Paralegals handle many routine assignments, particularly when they are inexperienced. They usually assume more responsible and varied tasks as they gain experience. Furthermore, as new laws and judicial interpretations emerge, paralegals are exposed to new legal problems that make their work more interesting and challenging.

*E*mployment

Paralegals held about 136,000 jobs in 1998. Private law firms employed the vast majority; most of the remainder worked for the various levels of government. Within the federal government, the Department of Justice is the largest employer of paralegals, followed by the Departments of Treasury and Defense and the Federal Deposit Insurance Corporation. Other employers include state and local governments, publicly funded legal service projects, banks, real estate development companies, and insurance companies. A small number of paralegals own their own businesses; as freelance legal assistants, they contract their services to attorneys or corporate legal departments.

*T*raining, Other Qualifications, and Advancement

There are several ways to become a paralegal. Employers generally require formal paralegal training obtained through associate or bachelor's degree programs or certificate programs. Increasingly, employers prefer graduates of four-year paralegal programs or college graduates who have completed short-term paralegal certificate programs. However, the majority of paralegals hold associate degrees. Some employers prefer to train paralegals on the job, promoting experienced legal secretaries or hiring college graduates with no legal experience. Other entrants have experience in a technical field that is useful to law firms, such as a background in tax preparation for tax and estate practice or nursing or health administration for personal injury practice.

Over 800 formal paralegal training programs are offered by four-year colleges and universities, law schools, community and junior colleges, business schools, and proprietary schools. There are currently 232 programs approved by the American Bar Association (ABA). Although this approval is neither required nor sought by many programs, graduation from an ABA-approved program can enhance one's employment opportunities. The requirements for admission to formal training programs vary widely. Some require some college courses or a bachelor's degree; others accept high school graduates or applicants with legal experience; and a few schools require standardized tests and personal interviews.

Paralegal programs include two-year associate degree programs, four-year bachelor's degree programs, and certificate programs that take only a few months to complete. Many certificate programs only require a high school diploma or general equivalency diploma (GED) for admission. Paralegal training programs typically include general courses on the law and legal research techniques, in addition to courses covering specialized areas of the law, such as real estate, estate planning and probate, litigation, family law, contracts, and criminal law. Many employers prefer applicants with specialized training. Programs increasingly include courses introducing students to the legal applications of computers. Many paralegal training programs include an internship in which students gain practical experience by working for several months in a law office, a corporate legal department, or a government agency. Experience gained in internships is an asset when seeking a job after graduation.

The quality of paralegal training programs varies; the better programs generally emphasize job placement. Prospective students should examine the experiences of recent graduates of programs in which they are considering enrolling.

Paralegals need not be certified, but the National Association of Legal Assistants has established standards for voluntary certification requiring various combinations of education and experience. Paralegals who meet these standards are eligible to take a two-day examination, given three times each year at several regional testing centers. Those who pass this examination may use the designation Certified Legal Assistant (CLA). This designation is a sign of competence in the field and may enhance employment and advancement opportunities. The Paralegal Advanced Competency Exam, established in 1996 and administered through the National Federation of Paralegal Associations, offers professional recognition to paralegals with a bachelor's degree and at least two years of experience. Those who pass this examination may use the designation Registered Paralegal (RP).

Paralegals must be able to handle legal problems logically and must be able to communicate, both orally and in writing, their findings and opinions to their supervising attorney. They must understand legal terminology and have good research and investigative skills. Familiarity with the operation and applications of computers in legal research and litigation support is increasingly important. Paralegals must always stay abreast of new developments in the law that affect their area of practice. Paralegals can participate in continuing legal education seminars to maintain their legal knowledge.

Because paralegals often deal with the public, they must be courteous and must uphold the high ethical standards of the legal profession. The National Association of Legal Assistants, the National Federation of Paralegal Associations, and a few states have established ethical guidelines that paralegals must follow.

Paralegals are usually given more responsibilities and less supervision as they gain work experience. In large law firms, corporate legal departments, and government agencies, experienced paralegals may supervise other paralegals and clerical staff and may delegate work assigned by the attorneys. Advancement opportunities include promotion to managerial and other law-related positions within the firm or corporate legal department. However, some paralegals find it easier to move to another law firm when seeking increased responsibility or advancement.

Job Outlook

Competition for jobs will continue as the growing number of graduates from paralegal education programs keeps pace with employment growth. Nevertheless, employment of paralegals is expected to grow much faster than average—ranking among the fastest-growing occupations in the economy through the year 2008—as law firms and other employers with legal staffs increasingly hire paralegals to lower the cost and to increase the availability and efficiency of legal services. While new jobs created by rapid employment growth will create most of the job openings for paralegals in the future, other job openings will arise as people leave the occupation.

Private law firms will continue to be the largest employers of paralegals as a growing population requires additional legal services, especially in areas such as intellectual property, health care law, international law, elder law, sexual harassment, and the environment. The growth of prepaid legal plans should also contribute to the demand for the services of law firms. A growing array of other organizations, such as corporate legal departments, insurance companies, real estate and title insurance firms, and banks, will also hire paralegals.

Job opportunities for paralegals will expand even in the public sector. Community legal service programs—which provide assistance to the poor, the aged, minorities, and middle-income families—operate on limited budgets. They will seek to employ additional paralegals to minimize expenses and to serve the most people. Federal, state, and local government agencies, consumer organizations, and the courts will continue to hire paralegals in increasing numbers.

To a limited extent, paralegal jobs are affected by the business cycle. During recessions, demand declines for some discretionary legal services, such as planning estates, drafting wills, and handling real estate transactions. Corporations are less inclined to initiate litigation when falling sales and profits lead to fiscal belt-tightening. As a result, full-time paralegals employed in offices adversely affected by a recession may be laid off or may have their work hours reduced. On the other hand, corporations and individuals are more likely to face other legal problems during recessions, such as bankruptcies, foreclosures, and divorces, that require legal assistance. Paralegals, who provide many of the same legal services at a lower cost, may fare better than lawyers.

$\mathcal{E}$arnings

Earnings of paralegals vary greatly. Salaries depend on education, training, experience, the type and size of the employer, and the geographic location of the job. Generally, paralegals who work for large law firms or in large metropolitan areas earn more than those who work for smaller firms or in less populated regions.

In 1998, full-time wage and salary paralegals had median annual earnings of $32,760. The middle 50% earned between $26,240 and 40,960. The top 10% earned more than $50,290, while the bottom 10% earned less than $21,770. Median annual earnings in the industries employing the largest numbers of paralegals in 1997 are shown below.

Federal government	$43,900
Local government	32,200
Legal services	30,300

According to the National Association of Legal Assistants, paralegals had an average salary of $34,000 in 1997. In addition to a salary, many paralegals received a bonus, which averaged about $2,100. According to the National Federation of Paralegal Associations, starting salaries of paralegals with one year or less experience averaged $30,700 in 1997.

Related Occupations

Several other occupations call for a specialized understanding of the law and the legal system but do not require the extensive training of a lawyer. Some of these are abstractors, claim examiners, compliance and enforcement inspectors, occupational safety and health workers, patent agents, police officers, and title examiners.

Sources of Additional Information

General information on a career as a paralegal can be obtained from

Standing Committee on Legal Assistants
American Bar Association
750 North Lake Shore Dr.
Chicago, IL 60611
Internet: http://www.abanet.org/legalassts

For information on the Certified Legal Assistant exam, schools that offer training programs in a specific state, and standards and guidelines for paralegals, contact

National Association of Legal Assistants, Inc.
1516 South Boston St., Suite 200
Tulsa, OK 74119
Internet: http://www.nala.org

Information on a career as a paralegal, schools that offer training programs, job postings for paralegals, the Paralegal Advanced Competency Exam, and local paralegal associations is available from

National Federation of Paralegal Associations
P.O. Box 33108
Kansas City, MO 64114
Internet: http://www.paralegals.org

Information on paralegal training programs, including the pamphlet "How to Choose a Paralegal Education Program," can be obtained from

American Association for Paralegal Education
P.O. Box 40244
Overland Park, KS 66204
Internet: http://www.aafpe.org

Information on acquiring a job as a paralegal specialist with the federal government can be obtained from the Office of Personnel Management through a telephone-based system. Consult your telephone directory under "U.S. Government" for a local number, or call (912) 757-3000; TDD (912) 744-2299. These numbers are not toll free, and charges may result. Information is also available from the Office of Personnel Management's Internet site: http://www.usajobs.opm.gov.

CHAPTER 9

Working as a Law Enforcement Officer

Significant Points

- Police work can be dangerous and stressful.
- The number of qualified candidates exceeds the number of job openings in federal and state law enforcement agencies but is inadequate to meet growth and replacement needs in many local and special police departments.
- The largest number of employment opportunities will arise in urban communities with relatively low salaries and high crime rates.

The material in this chapter is adapted from Bureau of Labor Statistics, U.S. Department of Labor, *Occupational Outlook Handbook*, 2000-01 Edition, Bulletin 2520. Superintendent of Documents, U.S. Government Printing Office, Washington, D.C., 2000.

Nature of the Work

The safety and well-being of our nation's citizens greatly depend on the police officers, detectives, and special agents responsible for enforcing statutes, laws, and regulations. Duties vary widely by the size and type of organization, but in most jurisdictions, whether on or off duty, law enforcement officers are expected to exercise their authority whenever necessary. And regardless of where they work or what they do, police officers, detectives, and special agents must spend considerable time writing the reports and maintaining the records that are needed when legal actions require them to testify in court.

Police officers who work in small communities and rural areas have general law enforcement duties. In the course of a day's work, they may direct traffic at the scene of a fire, investigate a burglary, or give first aid to an accident victim. In large police departments, by contrast, officers are usually assigned to a specific type of duty. Most officers are detailed to patrol a designated area to prevent crime. Patrols generally cover such areas as business districts or outlying residential neighborhoods. Officers may work alone, but in large agencies they usually patrol with a partner. They attempt to become thoroughly familiar with conditions throughout their patrol area and, while on patrol, remain alert for anything unusual. They note suspicious circumstances, such as open windows or lights in vacant buildings, as well as hazards to public safety. They identify, pursue, and arrest suspected criminals, resolve problems within the community, and enforce traffic laws. Officers are becoming more involved in community policing—building partnerships with the residents of local neighborhoods and mobilizing them to help fight crime.

Some police officers specialize and become experts in chemical and microscopic analysis or firearms, handwriting, or fingerprint identification. Others may work with special units, such as mounted or motorcycle patrol, harbor patrol, canine corps, special weapons and tactics or emergency response teams, or task forces formed to combat specific types of crime.

Detectives and *special agents* are plainclothes investigators who gather facts and collect evidence for criminal cases. They conduct interviews, examine records, observe the activities of suspects, and participate in raids or arrests.

Some local departments provide security officers, sometimes called "bailiffs," to maintain order in courtrooms.

Sheriffs and *deputy sheriffs* enforce the law on the county level. In metropolitan areas where there are also municipal police departments, the sheriffs' department may perform specialized duties, such as serving legal documents or operating the jail. A sheriff's duties resemble those of a local or county police chief, but the department is generally smaller. Most sheriffs' departments employ fewer than 25 sworn officers, and many employ fewer than 10.

State police officers (sometimes called "state troopers" or "highway patrol officers") patrol highways and enforce motor vehicle laws and regulations. They issue traffic citations to motorists who violate the law. At the scene of an accident, they may direct traffic, give first aid, and call for emergency equipment. They also write reports that may be used to determine the cause of the accident. In addition, state police officers may provide services to motorists, such as calling for road service for drivers with mechanical trouble.

State police officers also enforce criminal laws. They are frequently called upon to render assistance to officers of other law enforcement agencies. In rural areas that do not have a police force or a local deputy from the sheriff's department, the state police are the primary law enforcement agency, investigating any crimes that occur, such as burglary or assault.

The federal government maintains a high profile in many areas of law enforcement. *Federal Bureau of Investigation (FBI) special agents* are the government's principal investigators, responsible for investigating violations of more than 260 statutes. Agents may conduct surveillance, monitor court-authorized wiretaps, examine business records to investigate white-collar crime, track the interstate movement of stolen

property, collect evidence of espionage activities, or participate in sensitive undercover assignments. *Drug Enforcement
Administration (DEA) special agents* specialize in the enforcement of drug laws and regulations. Agents may conduct complex criminal investigations, carry out surveillance of
criminals, and infiltrate illicit drug organizations using
undercover techniques. *U.S. marshals* and *deputy marshals*
provide security for federal courts, including judges, witnesses, and prisoners, and apprehend fugitives. *U.S. Border
Patrol special agents* are responsible for protecting more than
8,000 miles of international land and water boundaries. Their
primary mission is to detect and prevent the smuggling and
unlawful entry of undocumented aliens into the United States
and to apprehend violators of the immigration laws. *Immigration and Naturalization Service (INS) agents* facilitate the
entry of legal visitors and immigrants to the United States and
detain and deport those arriving illegally.

Special agents employed by the U.S. Department of the
Treasury work for the Bureau of Alcohol, Tobacco, and
Firearms, the U.S. Customs Service, the Internal Revenue
Service, and the U.S. Secret Service. *Bureau of Alcohol,
Tobacco, and Firearms special agents* investigate violations of
federal firearms and explosives laws, as well as federal alcohol
and tobacco regulations. *Customs agents* inspect cargo, collect appropriate duties or fees, intercept contraband, and
ensure that all goods entering the United States comply with
U.S. laws and regulations. *Internal Revenue Service special
agents* collect evidence against individuals and companies
suspected of evading the payment of federal taxes. *U.S. Secret
Service special agents* protect the president and vice president
and their immediate families, presidential candidates, former
presidents, and foreign dignitaries visiting the United States.
Secret Service agents also investigate counterfeiting, the
forgery of government checks or bonds, and the fraudulent
use of credit cards.

Various other federal agencies employ police and special
agents with sworn arrest powers and the authority to carry
firearms. These agencies include the U.S. Forest Service
under the Department of Agriculture, the National Park Service under the Department of the Interior, and federal air

marshals under the Department of Transportation. Other police agencies generally evolved from the need for security for the agency's property and personnel. The largest such agency is the General Services Administration's Federal Protective Service, which provides security for federal buildings and property nationwide.

Working Conditions

Police work can be very dangerous and stressful. In addition to the obvious dangers of confrontations with criminals, the need to be constantly alert and ready to deal appropriately with any situation can be very stressful. Police officers, detectives, and special agents usually work a 40-hour week, but paid overtime work is common. Shift work is necessary because police protection must be provided around the clock. Junior officers frequently must work weekends, holidays, and nights. Police officers, detectives, and special agents are subject to call whenever their services are needed, and they may work long hours during investigations. All law enforcement officers are required to file reports of their activities, often involving long hours of paperwork. In most jurisdictions, whether on or off duty, officers are expected to be armed and to exercise their arrest authority whenever necessary.

The jobs of some federal agents, such as U.S. Secret Service and DEA special agents, require extensive travel, often on very short notice. These agents frequently relocate a number of times over the course of their career. Some police officers, detectives, and special agents with the U.S. Border Patrol and other agencies must work outdoors for long periods in all kinds of weather.

Employment

Police officers, detectives, and special agents held about 727,000 jobs in 1998. About 81% of police detectives and investigators were employed by local governments, primarily in cities with more than 25,000 inhabitants. Some cities have very large police forces, while hundreds of small communities employ fewer than 25 officers each. State police agencies employed about 13% of all police officers, detectives, and investigators; various federal agencies employed the other 6%.

Training, Other Qualifications, and Advancement

Civil service regulations govern the appointment of police officers and detectives in practically all state and large city agencies and in many smaller ones. Candidates must be U.S. citizens, must usually be at least 20 years of age, and must meet rigorous physical and personal qualifications. Eligibility for appointment generally depends on performance in competitive written examinations as well as on education and experience. Physical examinations often include tests of vision, hearing, strength, and agility.

Because personal characteristics such as honesty, judgment, integrity, and a sense of responsibility are especially important in law enforcement work, candidates are interviewed by senior officers, and their character traits and background are investigated. In some agencies, candidates are interviewed by a psychiatrist or a psychologist or are given a personality test. Most applicants are subjected to lie detector examinations and drug testing. Some agencies subject sworn personnel to random drug testing as a condition of continuing employment. Although police officers, detectives, and special agents work independently, they must perform their duties in accordance with the law and departmental rules. They should enjoy working with people and meeting the public.

In larger police departments, where the majority of law enforcement jobs are found, applicants usually must have at least a high school education. Federal agencies generally require a college degree. A few police departments accept applicants as recruits who have less than a high school education, but that number is declining.

The federal agency with the largest number of special agents is the FBI. To be considered for appointment as an FBI special agent, an applicant must be a graduate of an accredited law school, a college graduate with a major in accounting, or a college graduate with either fluency in a foreign language or three years of full-time work experience. All new agents undergo 16 weeks of training at the FBI academy on the U.S. Marine Corps base in Quantico, Virginia.

Applicants for special agent jobs with the U.S. Department of Treasury's Secret Service and the Bureau of Alcohol, Tobacco, and Firearms must have a bachelor's degree or a minimum of three years' work experience which demonstrates the ability to deal effectively with individuals or groups, among other things. Prospective special agents undergo eight weeks of training at the Federal Law Enforcement Training Center in Glynco, Georgia, and another 17 weeks of specialized training with their particular agencies.

Applicants for special agent jobs with the DEA must have a college degree and must have either one year of experience conducting criminal investigations, one year of graduate school, or at least a 2.95 grade point average while in college. DEA special agents undergo 14 weeks of specialized training at the FBI Academy in Quantico, Virginia.

Police departments are encouraging applicants to take postsecondary school training in law enforcement. Many applicants for entry-level police jobs have completed some formal postsecondary education, and a significant number are college graduates. In 1993, the most recent year for which data are available, 12% of local police departments required new officer recruits to have at least some college education. Many junior colleges, four-year colleges, and universities offer programs in law enforcement or administration of justice. Other courses helpful in preparing for a career in law enforcement include accounting, finance, electrical engineering or computer science, and foreign languages. Physical education and sports are helpful in developing the courage, competitiveness, stamina, and agility needed for law enforcement work. Knowledge of a foreign language is an asset in many agencies.

Some large cities hire high school graduates who are still in their teens as police cadets or trainees. They do clerical work and attend classes and can be appointed to the regular force at the conclusion of their training, usually in one to two years, upon reaching the minimum age requirement.

Before their first assignments, officers usually go through a period of training. In state and large local departments, recruits get training in their agency's police academy, often for 12 to 14 weeks. In small agencies, recruits often attend a regional or state academy. Training includes classroom instruction in constitutional law and civil rights, state laws and local ordinances, and accident investigation. Recruits also receive training and supervised experience in patrol, traffic control, use of firearms, self-defense, first aid, and emergency response.

Police officers usually become eligible for promotion after a probationary period ranging from six months to three years. In a large department, promotion may enable an officer to become a detective or to specialize in one type of police work, such as laboratory analysis of evidence or working with juveniles. Promotion to corporal, sergeant, lieutenant, and captain is usually made according to the candidate's position on a promotion list, as determined by scores on a written examination and on-the-job performance.

Continuing training helps police officers, detectives, and special agents improve their job performance. Through police department academies, regional centers for public safety employees, and federal training centers, instructors provide annual training in defensive tactics, firearms, use-of-force policies, sensitivity and communications skills, crowd-control techniques, legal developments that affect law enforcement work, and advances in law enforcement equipment. Many agencies pay all or part of the tuition for officers who work toward degrees in criminal justice, police science, administration of justice, or public administration, and they pay higher salaries to those who earn these degrees.

Job Outlook

The opportunity for public service through law enforcement work is attractive to many. The job is challenging and involves much personal responsibility. Furthermore, in many agencies, law enforcement officers may retire with a pension after 20 or 25 years of service, allowing them to pursue a second career while still in their 40s. Because of relatively attractive salaries and benefits, the number of qualified candidates exceeds the number of job openings in federal law enforcement agencies and in most state, local, and special police departments—resulting in stricter hiring standards and greater selectivity by employers. Competition is expected to remain keen for the higher-paying jobs with state and federal agencies and with police departments in more affluent areas. Candidates who have military experience, college training in police science, or both should have the best opportunities. The greatest number of openings will be in those urban communities whose departments offer relatively low salaries and where the crime rate is relatively high.

The employment of police officers, detectives, and special agents is expected to increase faster than the average for all occupations through the year 2008. A more security-conscious society and concern about drug-related crimes will contribute to the increasing demand for police services. At the local and state levels, growth is likely to continue as long as crime remains a serious concern. However, employment growth at the federal level will be tempered by the continuing budgetary constraints faced by law enforcement agencies. The turnover in police officer, detective, and special agent positions is among the lowest of all occupations; nevertheless, the need to replace workers who retire, transfer to other occupations, or stop working for other reasons will create the most job openings.

The level of government spending affects employment opportunities for police officers, detectives, and special agents. The number of job openings can vary from year to year and from place to place. Layoffs, on the other hand, are rare because retirements allow the occasional need for staff reductions to be met through attrition. Trained law enforcement officers who lose their jobs because of budget cuts usually have little difficulty finding jobs with other agencies.

*E*arnings

In 1998, the median salary of nonsupervisory police officers and detectives was about $48,700 a year. The middle 50% earned between about $37,130 and $48,700; the lowest 10% were paid less than $28,780, while the highest 10% earned over $84,710 a year.

Police officers and detectives in supervisory positions had a median salary of about $46,180 a year in 1998. The middle 50% earned between about $35,540 and $62,520; the lowest 10% were paid less than $27,950, while the highest 10% earned over $80,120 annually.

Sheriffs and other law enforcement officers had a median annual salary of about $28,270 in 1998. The middle 50% earned between about $23,310 and $36,090; the lowest 10% were paid less than $19,070, while the highest 10% earned over $44,420.

Federal law provides special salary rates to federal employees who serve in law enforcement. Additionally, federal special agents receive availability pay or administratively uncontrolled overtime (AUO)—equal to 25% of the agent's grade and step—awarded because of the large amount of overtime that these agents are expected to work. For example, in 1999, FBI agents started at a base salary of $34,400 a year, earning $43,000 a year with availability pay. Other Justice and Treasury Department special agents started at about $53,800 a year, earning $67,300 per year with availability pay, depending on their qualifications. Salaries of federal special agents progress to $79,500 with availability pay, while supervisory agents started at $93,500 with availability pay. Salaries were slightly higher in selected areas where the prevailing local pay level was higher. Because federal agents may be eligible for a special law enforcement benefits package, applicants should ask their recruiter for more information.

The International City-County Management Association's annual Police and Fire Personnel, Salaries, and Expenditures Survey revealed that 84% of the municipalities surveyed provided police services in 1997. The following salaries are for sworn full-time positions in 1997.

Police officer	$28,200–38,500
Police corporal	31,900–39,000
Police sergeant	38,200–45,100
Police lieutenant	42,900–51,200
Police captain	46,500–56,600
Deputy chief	48,400–59,800
Police chief	56,300–69,600

Total earnings for local, state, and special police officers and detectives frequently exceed the stated salary due to payments for overtime, which can be significant. In addition to the common benefits—paid vacation, sick leave, and medical and life insurance—most police and sheriffs' departments provide officers with special allowances for uniforms. In addition, because police officers generally are covered by liberal pension plans, many retire at half-pay after 20 or 25 years of service.

Related Occupations

Police officers, detectives, and special agents maintain law and order. Workers in related occupations include correctional officers, guards, fire marshals, and inspectors.

Sources of Additional Information

Information about entrance requirements can be obtained from federal, state, and local law enforcement agencies.

Information about qualifications for employment as an FBI special agent is available from state FBI offices; look in your local telephone directory for the address and phone number of the nearest state office, or visit the FBI's Web site (http://www.fbi.gov).

For information about qualifications for employment as a DEA special agent, write to the nearest DEA office, call (800) DEA-4288, or visit the DEA's Web site (http://www.usdoj.gov/dea).

Information about career opportunities, qualifications, and training to become a deputy marshal is available from

U.S. Marshals Service
Employment and Compensation Division
Field Staffing Branch
600 Army Navy Dr.
Arlington, VA 22202
Internet: http://www.usdoj.gov/marshals

Career opportunities, qualifications, and training for U.S. Secret Service special agents is available from

U.S. Secret Service
Personnel Division, Room 912
1800 G St. N.W.
Washington, DC 20223
Internet: http://www.ustreas.gov/usss

For information on career opportunities and Bureau of Alcohol, Tobacco, and Firearms operations, contact

U.S. Bureau of Alcohol, Tobacco, and Firearms
Personnel Division
650 Massachusetts Ave. N.W., Room 4170
Washington, DC 20226
Internet: http://www.atf.treas.gov

Information about careers with the U.S. Border Patrol is available from

U.S. Border Patrol
Chester A. Arthur Bldg.
425 I St. N.W.
Washington, DC 20536
Internet: http://www.ins.usdoj.gov/bpmain/index.htm

CHAPTER 10

Working as a Private Investigator

$\mathcal{S}$ignificant Points

- Work hours are often irregular for beginning detectives and investigators, many of whom work part-time.
- Most applicants have related experience in other areas, such as law enforcement, insurance, or the military.
- Stiff competition is expected for better-paying jobs because of the large number of qualified people who are attracted to this occupation.
- A license is required to work as a private investigator in most areas.

The material in this chapter is adapted from Bureau of Labor Statistics, U.S. Department of Labor, *Occupational Outlook Handbook*, 2000-01 Edition, Bulletin 2520. Superintendent of Documents, U.S. Government Printing Office, Washington, D.C., 2000.

Nature of the Work

Private detectives and investigators assist attorneys, businesses, and the public with a variety of problems. Their services include protecting businesses and their employees, customers, and guests from theft, vandalism, and disorder as well as gathering evidence for trials, tracing debtors, and conducting background investigations. Although detectives concentrate on providing protection and investigators specialize in gathering information, many do some of each.

The duties of private detectives and investigators range from locating missing persons to exposing fraudulent workers' compensation claims. Some specialize in one field, such as finance, where they might use accounting skills to investigate the financial standing of a company or to locate funds stolen by an embezzler. Others specialize in locating missing persons, investigating infidelity, or conducting background investigations, including financial profiles and asset searches; others do executive protection and bodyguard work.

Most detectives and investigators are trained to perform physical surveillance, often for long periods of time, in a car or van. They may observe a site, such as the home of a subject, from an inconspicuous location. The surveillance continues, using still and video cameras, binoculars, and a citizen's band radio or a car phone, until the desired evidence is obtained.

Many detectives and investigators perform online computer database searches or work with someone who does. Computers allow detectives and investigators to obtain massive amounts of information in a short period of time from the dozens of online databases containing probate records, motor vehicle registrations, credit reports, association membership lists, and other information.

Private detectives and investigators obtain information by interviewing witnesses and assembling evidence and reports for litigation or criminal trials. They get cases from clients or are assigned to cases by the manager of their firm. Many spend considerable time conducting surveillance, seeking to observe inconsistencies in a subject's behavior. For example, a person who has recently filed a workers' compensation claim stating that an injury has made walking difficult should not be able to jog or mow the lawn. If such behavior is observed, the investigator takes video or still photographs to document the activity and reports back to the supervisor or client.

Some investigations involve verification of facts, such as an individual's place of employment or income. This might involve a phone call or a visit to the workplace. In other investigations, especially in missing persons cases and background checks, the investigator interviews people to gather as much information as possible about the subject.

Legal investigators specialize in cases involving the courts and are normally employed by law firms or lawyers. They frequently assist in preparing criminal defenses, locate witnesses, interview police officers, gather and review evidence, take photographs, and testify in court. To assist attorneys in the preparation of civil litigation, they interview prospective witnesses, collect information on the parties to the litigation, and search for testimonial, documentary, or physical evidence.

Corporate investigators work for companies other than investigative firms—often large corporations. They conduct internal or external investigations. External investigations may consist of undercover operations aimed at preventing criminal schemes, thefts of company assets, or fraudulent deliveries of products by suppliers. In internal investigations, they may investigate drug use in the workplace, ensure that expense accounts are not abused, and determine whether employees are stealing merchandise or information.

Detectives and investigators who specialize in finance may be hired to develop confidential financial profiles of individuals or companies involved in large financial transactions, and they often work with investment bankers and accountants. They also may search for assets after fraud or theft to recover damages awarded by a court.

Private detectives and investigators who work for retail stores or malls are responsible for loss control and asset protection. *Store detectives* safeguard the assets of retail stores by apprehending anyone attempting to steal merchandise or to destroy store property. They detect theft by shoplifters, vendor representatives, delivery personnel, and even store employees. Store detectives also conduct periodic inspections of stock areas, dressing rooms, and rest rooms, and they sometimes assist in the opening and closing of the store. They may prepare loss-prevention and security reports for management and may testify in court against suspects they apprehend.

Working Conditions

Private detectives and investigators often work irregular hours because of the need to conduct surveillance and to contact people who are not available during normal working hours. Early morning, evening, weekend, and holiday work is common.

Many detectives and investigators spend much time away from their offices conducting interviews or doing surveillance, but some work in their office most of the day conducting computer searches and making phone calls. Some split their time between office and field. Those who have their own agencies and employ other investigators may work primarily in an office and have normal business hours.

When working a case away from the office, the environment might range from plush boardrooms to seedy bars. Store and hotel detectives work mostly in the businesses that they protect. Investigators generally work alone, but during surveillance or when following a subject, they may work with others.

Much of the work detectives and investigators do can be confrontational because the person being observed or interviewed may not want to be. As a result, the job can be stressful and sometimes dangerous. Some detectives and investigators carry handguns. In most cases, a weapon is not necessary because the purpose of the work is the gathering of information and not law enforcement or apprehension of criminals. Owners of investigative agencies have the added stress of having to deal with demanding and sometimes distraught clients.

*E*mployment

Nationwide, private detectives and investigators held about 61,000 jobs in 1998. About one in four was self-employed. About a third of wage and salary workers worked for detective agencies, and another third were employed as store detectives in department or clothing and accessories stores. The remainder worked for hotels and other lodging places, legal services firms, and in other industries.

*T*raining, Other Qualifications, and Advancement

There are no formal education requirements for most private detective and investigator jobs, although most employers prefer high school graduates, and many private detectives do have college degrees.

Training in subjects like criminal justice is helpful to the aspiring private detective or investigator. Most corporate investigators must have a bachelor's degree, preferably in a business-related field. Some corporate investigators have masters of business administration or law degrees, while others are certified public accountants.

Almost all private detectives and investigators have previous experience in other occupations. Retired law enforcement officers, military investigators, and government agents frequently become private detectives and investigators as a second career. Others enter from such diverse fields as finance, accounting, collections, investigative reporting, insurance, and law. These individuals can apply their prior work experience in a related investigation specialty. A few enter the occupation directly after graduation from college, generally with majors in such fields as criminal justice and police science.

Most states and the District of Columbia require private detectives and investigators to be licensed by the state or local authorities. Licensing requirements vary widely. Some states have very liberal requirements or none at all, while others have stringent regulations. For example, the California Department of Consumer Affairs Bureau of Security and Investigative Services requires 6,000 hours of investigative experience, a background check, and a qualifying score on a written examination. A growing number of states are enacting mandatory training programs for private detectives and investigators. In most states, convicted felons may not be licensed.

In most investigations firms, the screening process for potential employees includes a background check to confirm education and work experience, to inquire about criminal history, and to interview references and others who know the applicant.

For private detective and investigator jobs, most employers look for individuals with ingenuity who are curious, aggressive, persistent, and assertive. A candidate must not be afraid of being confrontational, should communicate well, and should be able to think on his or her feet. The courts are often the ultimate judge of a properly conducted investigation, so the investigator must be able to present the facts in a manner that a jury will believe.

Corporate investigators hired by larger companies may receive formal training from their employers on business practices, management structure, and various finance-related topics. Good interviewing and interrogation skills are important. Most investigators usually acquire these skills in earlier careers in law enforcement or other fields.

Most investigation firms are small, with little room for advancement. Usually, there are no defined ranks or steps, so advancement is in terms of salary and assignment status. Many detectives and investigators work for various investigation firms at the beginning of their careers and after a few years try to start their own firms. Corporate and legal investigators may rise to supervisor or manager of the security or investigations department.

Job Outlook

The employment of private detectives and investigators is expected to grow faster than average for all occupations through the year 2008. In addition, job turnover will create many additional job openings, particularly among wage and salary workers. Nevertheless, competition is expected for the available openings due to the attractiveness of private detective and investigator careers and to the number of young law enforcement and military retirees who are qualified to enter the field.

Increased demand for private detectives and investigators is expected to be generated by fear of crime, increased litigation, and the need to protect confidential information and property of all kinds. Law firms will need additional private investigators to meet the needs for criminal defense and civil litigation among companies and individuals. Greater corporate financial activity worldwide will increase the demand for investigators to control internal and external financial losses, as well as to find out what competitors are doing and to prevent industrial spying.

Opportunities will be best for entry-level jobs as store detectives and for part-time jobs with detective agencies. Those seeking store detective jobs may find the best opportunities with private guard and security firms since some retail businesses are replacing their own workers with outside contract workers.

Earnings

The earnings of private detectives and investigators vary greatly depending on their employer, their specialty, and the geographic area in which they work. According to a study by Abbott, Langer & Associates, security/loss prevention directors and vice presidents earned an average $65,500 a year in 1998, investigators about $49,300 a year, and store detectives about $17,700.

Most private investigators bill their clients between $50 and $150 per hour to conduct investigations. Except for those working for large corporations, most private investigators do not receive paid vacation or sick days, health or life insurance, retirement packages, or other benefits. Investigators are usually reimbursed for expenses and generally receive a car allowance. Most corporate investigators received health insurance, pension plans, profit-sharing plans, and paid vacation.

Related Occupations

Private detectives and investigators often collect information and protect property and company assets. Others with related concerns include security guards, insurance claims examiners, inspectors, collectors, and law enforcement officers. Investigators who specialize in conducting financial profiles and asset searches do work that is closely related to that of accountants and financial analysts.

Sources of Additional Information

For information on local licensing requirements, contact your state department of public safety, state division of licensing, or local or state police headquarters.

Information on a career as a legal investigator is available from

National Association of Legal Investigators
P.O. Box 905
Grand Blanc, MI 48439
Internet: http://www.nali.com/index.htm

CHAPTER 11

Working as a Private Security Officer

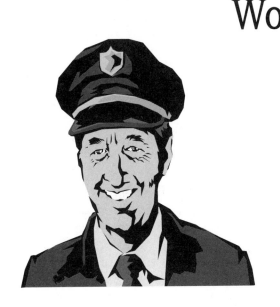

*S*ignificant Points

- Favorable opportunities are expected for lower-paying jobs, but stiff competition is likely for higher-paying positions at facilities requiring a high level of security, such as nuclear plants and government installations.
- Many employers of unarmed security personnel do not have any specific educational requirements, although employers generally will not hire applicants who have been convicted of a serious crime.
- Some positions, such as armored car guard, are hazardous.
- Because of limited formal training requirements and flexible hours, this occupation attracts many individuals seeking a second part-time job.

The material in this chapter is adapted from Bureau of Labor Statistics, U.S. Department of Labor, *Occupational Outlook Handbook*, 2000-01 Edition, Bulletin 2520. Superintendent of Documents, U.S. Government Printing Office, Washington, D.C., 2000.

*N*ature of the Work

Security officers patrol and inspect property to protect against fire, theft, vandalism, and illegal entry. Their duties vary with the size, type, and location of their employer. (Correctional officers—security personnel who work in prisons and other correctional institutions—and law enforcement officers are discussed in Chapters 5 and 9.)

In office buildings, banks, hospitals, and department stores, guards protect people, records, merchandise, money, and equipment. In department stores, they often work with undercover detectives to watch for theft by customers or store employees.

At air, sea, and rail terminals and other transportation facilities, private security personnel protect people, merchandise being shipped, property, and equipment. They screen passengers and visitors for weapons, explosives, and other contraband, ensure that nothing is stolen while being loaded or unloaded, and watch for fires and prowlers. They may direct traffic.

Security officers who work in public buildings, such as museums or art galleries, protect paintings and exhibits by inspecting the people and packages entering and leaving the building. They answer routine questions from visitors and sometimes guide tours.

In factories, laboratories, government buildings, data-processing centers, and military bases in which valuable property or information—such as new product information, computer codes, or defense secrets—must be protected, private security personnel check the credentials of people and vehicles entering and leaving the premises. University, park, and recreation guards perform similar duties and also may issue parking permits and direct traffic. Golf course patrollers prevent unauthorized people from using the facility and help keep play running smoothly.

At social affairs, sports events, conventions, and other public gatherings, private security personnel provide information, assist in crowd control, and watch for people who may cause trouble. Some guards patrol places of entertainment, such as nightclubs, to preserve order among customers and to protect property.

Armored car guards protect money and valuables during transit. Bodyguards protect individuals from bodily injury, kidnapping, or invasion of privacy.

In a large organization, a security officer is often in charge of the guard force; in a small organization, a single worker may be responsible for all security measures. Patrolling is usually done on foot, but if the property is large, private security personnel may make their rounds by car or motor scooter. As more businesses purchase advanced electronic security systems to protect their property, more guards are being assigned to stations where they monitor perimeter security, environmental functions, communications, and other systems. In many cases, these guards maintain radio contact with other guards patrolling on foot or in motor vehicles. Some private security personnel use computers to store information on matters relevant to security—for example, visitors or suspicious occurrences—during their hours on duty.

As they make their rounds, security personnel check all doors and windows, see that no unauthorized people remain after working hours, and ensure that fire extinguishers, alarms, sprinkler systems, furnaces, and various electrical and plumbing systems are working properly.

Private security personnel who carry weapons must be licensed by the appropriate government authority, and some receive further certification as special police officers, which allows them to make limited types of arrests while on duty. Unarmed security personnel may carry a flashlight, a whistle, a two-way radio, and a watch clock—a device that indicates the time at which they reach various checkpoints.

Working Conditions

Most security personnel spend considerable time on their feet patrolling buildings, industrial plants, and grounds. Indoors, they may be stationed at a guard desk to monitor electronic security and surveillance devices or to check the credentials of people entering or leaving the premises. They also may be stationed at a gate or may patrol grounds in all weather.

Because some guards work alone, especially at night, there may be no one nearby to help if an accident or injury occurs. Many security personnel use a portable radio or telephone that allows them to be in constant contact with a central station outside the guarded area. If they fail to transmit an expected signal, the central station investigates. Guard work is usually routine, but guards must be constantly alert for threats to themselves and to the property they are protecting. Private security personnel who work during the day may have extensive contact with other employees and with members of the public.

Many private security personnel work alone at night; the usual shift lasts eight hours. Some employers have three shifts, and guards rotate to divide daytime, weekend, and holiday work equally. Guards usually eat on the job instead of taking a regular break away from the site.

Employment

Private security personnel held over one million jobs in 1998. Industrial security firms and guard agencies employed 60% of all such workers. These organizations provide security services on contract, assigning their guards to buildings and other sites as needed. The remainder were in-house security personnel employed in many settings, including banks, building management companies, hotels, hospitals, retail stores, restaurants, bars, schools, and government. Private security jobs are found throughout the country, mostly in metropolitan areas.

Training, Other Qualifications, and Advancement

Most states require that private security personnel be licensed. To be licensed as a guard, individuals must generally be 18 years old, pass a background examination, and complete classroom training in such subjects as property rights, emergency procedures, and the detention of suspected criminals.

Many employers of unarmed guards do not have any specific educational requirements. For armed security personnel, employers generally prefer individuals who are high school graduates. Some jobs require a driver's license. For positions as armed security personnel, employers often seek people who have had experience in the military or in law enforcement. Most people entering guard jobs have prior work experience, although it is usually unrelated. Because of limited formal training requirements and flexible hours, this occupation attracts some people seeking a second job.

Applicants are expected to have good character references, no serious police record, good health—especially hearing and vision—and good personal habits, such as neatness and dependability. They should be mentally alert, emotionally stable, and physically fit in order to cope with emergencies. Security personnel who have frequent contact with the public should be friendly and personable. Some employers require applicants to undergo a polygraph examination or a psychological profile. Many employers require applicants and experienced workers to submit to drug-screening tests as a condition of employment.

Candidates for guard jobs in the federal government must have some experience as a guard and must pass a written examination in order to be certified by the General Services Administration. Armed forces experience is an asset. For most federal guard positions, applicants must qualify in the use of firearms.

The amount of training private security personnel receive varies. Training requirements are higher for armed guards because their employers are legally responsible for any use of force. Armed guards receive formal training in areas such as weapons use and retention and laws covering the use of force.

Many employers give newly hired personnel instruction before they start the job and also provide several weeks of on-the-job training. An increasing number of states are making ongoing training a legal requirement for retention of certification. Security personnel may receive training in protection, public relations, report writing, crisis deterrence, and first aid, as well as specialized training relevant to their particular assignment.

Private security personnel employed at establishments placing a heavy emphasis on security usually receive extensive formal training. For example, guards at nuclear power plants undergo several months of training before being placed on duty under close supervision. They are taught to use firearms, administer first aid, operate alarm systems and electronic security equipment, and spot and deal with security problems. Private security personnel authorized to carry firearms may be periodically tested in their use. Some security personnel are likewise periodically tested for health, strength, and endurance.

Although guards in small companies receive periodic salary increases, advancement is limited. However, most large organizations use a military type of ranking that offers the possibility of advancement in position and salary. Guards with talent and some college education may advance to jobs that involve administrative and management duties. Security personnel with management skills may open their own contract security guard agencies.

Job Outlook

Job opportunities for private security personnel are expected to be very favorable through the year 2008. High turnover and this occupation's large size rank it among those providing the greatest number of job openings in the economy. Many opportunities are expected for people seeking full-time employment, as well as for those seeking part-time or second jobs at night or on weekends. However, some competition is expected for higher-paying, high-security positions. Compared to unarmed security guards, armed security personnel and special police enjoy higher earnings and benefits, greater job security, and more advancement potential and are usually given more training and responsibility.

Employment of private security personnel is expected to grow faster than the average for all occupations through the year 2008. Increased concern about crime, vandalism, and terrorism will heighten the need for security in and around homes, plants, stores, offices, and recreation areas. Demand for guards will also grow as private security firms increasingly perform duties formerly handled by government police officers and marshals, such as monitoring crowds at airports and providing security in courts. Because engaging the services of a security guard firm is easier and less costly than assuming direct responsibility for hiring, training, and managing a security guard force, job growth is expected to be concentrated among contract security guard agencies.

Private security personnel employed by industrial security and guard agencies are occasionally laid off when the firm at which they work does not renew its contract with their agency. Most are able to find employment with other agencies, however, and may even continue to work at the same location for the firm that won the contract. Guards employed directly by the firm at which they work are seldom laid off because a plant or factory must still be protected even when economic conditions force it to close temporarily.

Earnings

Median annual earnings of private security personnel who worked full-time in guard positions in 1998 were about $16,240. The middle 50% earned between $13,430 and $20,110. The lowest 10% earned less than $11,970, and the highest 10% earned more than $26,640. Guards generally earn slightly more in urban areas.

Median annual earnings in the industries employing the largest numbers of guards in 1997 are shown below.

Real estate operators and lessors	$20,300
Hospitals	19,500
Hotels and motels	18,000

| Miscellaneous amusement and recreation services | 15,800 |
| Miscellaneous business services | 14,800 |

Depending on their experience, newly hired security personnel in the federal government earned $16,400 or $18,400 a year in 1999. Beginning salaries were slightly higher in selected areas where the prevailing local pay level was higher. Guards employed by the federal government averaged about $26,300 a year in 1999. These workers usually receive overtime pay as well as a wage differential for the second and third shifts.

Related Occupations

Private security personnel protect property, maintain security, and enforce regulations for entry and conduct in the establishments at which they work. Related security and protective service occupations include bailiffs, correctional officers, house and store detectives, and private investigators.

Sources of Additional Information

Further information about work opportunities for private security personnel is available from local detective and security firms and from state employment service offices.

Information about licensing requirements for private security personnel may be obtained from the state licensing commission or the state police department. In states where local jurisdictions establish licensing requirements, contact the local government authority, such as the sheriff, county executive, or city manager.

CHAPTER 12

Career Information on the World Wide Web

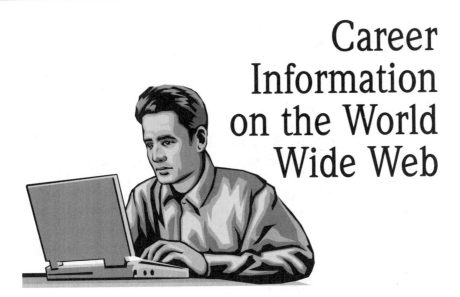

$\mathcal{S}$ignificant Points

- Finding employment through online sources is easier than traveling a long way to investigate local job markets.
- A number of free employment services can be found on the Web, many of which list jobs in the criminal justice and public safety field.
- Career advice and résumé-posting services enhance the value of the Web for job-seekers.

The material in this chapter is adapted from Bureau of Labor Statistics, U.S. Department of Labor, *Occupational Outlook Handbook*, 2000-01 Edition, Bulletin 2520. Superintendent of Documents, U.S. Government Printing Office, Washington, D.C., 2000.

Finding Employment Online

Not long ago, finding a job required a lot of legwork. Job-seekers had to read newspapers, subscribe to special employment services, and sometimes travel considerable distances to investigate local job markets. Although applying for a job today is still one of the most daunting experiences facing recent college graduates, the process has been made a lot easier by online job banks and electronic employment services.

Some sites, such as Government Jobs.Com, are designed to make your job search efficient. No fees are charged to search the site. Although the site is private, government agencies—including those at the federal, state, and local levels—frequently post job openings. Job search firms and advertising agencies also advertise vacant positions through the service. Although employers must pay a fee to advertise, potential employees can search all job vacancies for free.

Each Government Jobs.Com listing includes the position title, a description of the position, job requirements (education, special skills, etc.), duties and responsibilities, salary if given, closing date, name of agency, and any other information pertinent to the position. In addition to job listings, Government Jobs.Com provides job resource information by state, including job-line phone numbers, city and county leagues and associations, statewide newspapers, and so forth. It also includes links to municipal and county government Web sites.

The federal government maintains a number of job-listing services on the Web and uses such sites as recruitment tools. One of the most popular is FedWorld (you can reach the jobs page at http://www.fedworld.gov/jobs/jobsearch.html). If you visit FedWorld, you can also click on a selection that reads "Sign up to get FedWorld Vacancy Announcements via Email." Fill out the form that appears, send it to the FedWorld server, and you will quickly find job announcements appearing in your e-mail box. FedWorld also makes available some shareware software packages containing federal job application forms OF612 and SF171, which many people use to apply for federal jobs.

Some agencies are now posting job application forms directly on the Web. You can complete these forms online, click the "Submit" button at the end of the form, and apply for a job without ever leaving your computer. An application form for employment as a U.S. Border Patrol agent, for example, is available online at http://www.usajobs.opm.gov /BPA1.HTM.

Significantly, a number of criminal justice-specific sites offer a wide range of useful services. Notable among these is AdviseNet(c). AdviseNet (http://courses.smsu.edu/mkc096f) bills itself as "the incredible online criminal justice adviser." As its name implies, this site offers advice as well as other services. Although its primary target is students studying in or graduating from university-level criminal justice programs, it is a useful site for any college student, regardless of major. AdviseNet contains over 175 folders of information and 2,400 links to sites and documents, but it is designed to be navigated quickly.

The AdviseNet main menu consists of three major categories: "Getting Started," "Studying Criminal Justice," and "Life after Graduation." The "Getting Started" section offers students tips on how to get better grades, write better term papers, make a good impression in class, succeed in other aspects of university life, and more.

In the "Studying Criminal Justice" category, you can find answers to such questions as whether a student needs to major or minor in criminal justice to succeed in that field, what other majors, minors, and non-criminal justice courses may be useful to take, and where to find and obtain research data on crime and justice. It also includes links to a variety of issues and important sites related to criminal justice.

The section titled "Life after Graduation" offers users information on careers in criminal justice, including descriptions of many careers, search engines for finding job openings, links to professional associations, and a dynamic site on graduate study. If you're anticipating graduate study, be sure to visit this site! Links to every graduate criminal justice or criminology program in the United States are provided, along with insights on choosing thesis and dissertation topics, the degree committee, how to negotiate one's salary (for academics), and insider information about how academics earn tenure and get promoted.

Included in the "Life after Graduation" section are links to a variety of grant and funding agencies that specialize in supporting nonprofit efforts—particularly useful information for criminal justice graduates who end up working for nonprofit organizations.

Unlike most advising situations, students are able to access this online adviser, complete with e-mail contact, 24 hours a day, 365 days a year. Because it is maintained regularly, the advice and insights offered are up-to-date and timely. Information on the site is written in a style that is inviting and positive—drawing users into thinking about what they are doing at the university and how their college time may be best spent.

AdviseNet was created in 1996 by Dr. Mike Carlie, Professor of Sociology and Criminal Justice at Southwest Missouri State University, and he updates it regularly. Dr. Carlie has been teaching, conducting research, publishing, and serving the professional community since receiving his Ph.D. in Sociology from Washington University (St. Louis) in 1970. He served on the Criminal Justice Planning Agency, U.S. Department of Justice, and numerous community boards as a member and as an executive. He has been an intern supervisor and has been influential in the creation of several different university-level criminal justice programs since 1972. These experiences, and knowledge gained from having had over 25,000 students in his classroom over the years, inform the site and ensure that the user receives realistic advice. Check out Dr. Carlie's vitae on AdviseNet.

Job-Listing Services

This chapter presents job-listing services in three categories: (1) general listing services, (2) government-run or government-sponsored job sites, and (3) criminal justice-specific job-listing services. We'll start with general listing services.

GENERAL JOB-LISTING SERVICES

General job-listing services frequently provide up-to-date information on positions that are available *now*. They are a lot like "help wanted" sections in newspapers or trade journals. Some sites, however, provide much more, including résumé-posting services, career development guides, and tuition assistance information.

Among the most useful sites are those that allow employers to search for potential employees. If you are seeking employment, many of these sites help you prepare a résumé, advise you on how to submit it to agencies that are currently hiring, or post your résumé and credentials online for potential employers to see. You may want to consider posting your résumé online yourself and then directing potential employers to it. Doing so can demonstrate your technical and computer prowess. You can view the online résumé of Dr. Schmalleger, Director of the Justice Research Association, online at http://cjcentral.com/resume. Although it is unlikely that your résumé will be nearly as lengthy as Dr. Schmalleger's, this page should give you an idea of how to build your own online résumé.

Some of the best general job-listing services are described below. (Most services are free, but you may have to register online or join the sponsoring agency or association to gain full access to some sites.)

Career Builder
http://careerbuilder.com
This site has a great job-search feature that allows potential employees to search using criteria like salary, geographic region, type of job sought, and keywords.

Career Magazine
http://www.careermag.com
This is a comprehensive resource designed to meet the individual needs of networked job-seekers. More than just a job-search site, *Career* Magazine is just what its name implies—a Web-based e-magazine for job-seekers and employers.

CareerMart

http://www.careermart.com
CareerMart bills itself as "the most user-friendly employment site on the Web." With only a few clicks you can find job listings in your area of interest.

Career Mosaic

http://www.careermosaic.com
One of the oldest and most venerable job-search sites on the Web, Career Mosaic allows job-seekers to search according to a wide range of criteria and to receive e-mail notification when jobs of potential interest are posted to the site.

CareerNet

http://www.careers.org
At this site you will find over 11,000 links to jobs, employers, businesses, educational institutes, and career service professionals and over 6,000 links to employment-related resources.

CareerPath

http://www.careerpath.com
CareerPath provides users with access to thousands of job ads scanned from hundreds of newspapers across the country.

CareerSite

http://www.careersite.com
This free service permits employers to submit want ads to many different job boards. The site also serves as a tool to help employers manage responses. Job-seekers can post confidential résumés at the site.

CareerWeb

http://www.cweb.com
CareerWeb offers a free place to store your résumé online. It uses a job-match function to send you e-mail notification of jobs fitting your interests.

College Grad Job Hunter

http://www.collegegrad.com
Featured sections provide information on preparing for a
career and preparing for the job interview, writing a
résumé and cover letter, and negotiating a salary. Job postings and résumé postings are available.

Cool Works

http://www.coolworks.com/showme
The site says that you can "live and work where others
only visit." It lists 75,000 jobs in places like state and
national parks, camps, resorts, amusement parks, and ski
resorts. Many of the listings are for seasonal employment.

4Work

http://www.4work.com
This site allows you to screen thousands of Web-posted
jobs to find the one that's right for you. Job Alert!, a special feature of the site, is a confidential job-search agent
that screens thousands of jobs. You get results in approximately two minutes with fresh updates sent to your e-mail
box daily. Searches are free for job-seekers.

HeadHunter

http://www.headhunter.net
Although most general job-search sites charge employers
to post ads, HeadHunter is totally free to both employers
and employees. Both ads and résumés, however, can be
upgraded and made more visible for a fee.

Hot Jobs

http://www.hotjobs.com
Organized by category, the site provides lots of listings,
including jobs in Canada, Australia, and elsewhere. You
can search by keyword, company, or location.

Intellimatch

http://www.intellimatch.com
This service matches your résumé with the needs of
prospective employers.

JobDirect

http://www.jobdirect.com
This site focuses on linking college students and college graduates with potential employers. JobDirect TV streams video featuring potential employers to your desktop.

Job Hunt

http://www.job-hunt.org
Job Hunt offers specialized job listings, including those in academia, computers, engineering, accounting, consulting, and medicine. Visit the site's "Law and Law Enforcement" section at http://www.job-hunt.org/law.shtml.

Jobs.com

http://www.jobs.com
Find employment by zip code, category, or keywords. The site provides a wealth of career resources, including a résumé-writing tool and message boards.

JobTrak

http://www.jobtrak.com
This job-listing service, in partnership with hundreds of college and university career centers, is used by over 200,000 employers.

JobWeb

http://www.jobweb.org
This site offers lots of job-hunting tips, along with an employment outlook and an "online career fair."

The Monster Board

http://www.monster.com
PC Magazine (May 25, 1999) rates Monster.com the best online site for both job-seekers and employers. The "My Monster" personalization feature is highly customizable and allows job-seekers to create a number of résumés, cover letters, and job-search agents.

The Riley Guide

http://www.dbm.com/jobguide

This is a very comprehensive job-seeker's site with lots of
links to related services. The last time we checked, however, the interface was from the Web's stone age.

GOVERNMENT JOB SITES

America's Job Bank

http://www.ajb.dni.us

This totally free site offers a good résumé-creation facility,
job market information, and a powerful job search engine.
Run by the U.S. Department of Labor, the site has nearly
one million job listings and hosts a national database of
résumés in an area called America's Talent Bank.

Database of Government Jobs

http://www.govtjobs.com/crim/index.html

One of the latest and most up-to-date listings of state and
federal government job opportunities, this private (non-
government-run) site also provides job resource information by state.

**Department of Labor Employment and Training
Administration**

http://www.doleta.gov

The home page of the U.S. Depatment of Labor's Employment and Training Administration. The site includes job
listings for adults and juveniles, as well as employment
statistics for the nation.

**Federal Bureau of Investigation (FBI) Virtual
Employment Center**

http://www.fbi.gov/employment/virtvid.htm

Information on hiring, recruitment, salaries, and employment statistics at the FBI can be found here.

Federal Support Services

http://www.federalsupportservices.com/fssframe.html
This site tells visitors that the federal government employs
approximately 100,000 law enforcement personnel and
hires *hundreds*, even *thousands*, of people each year!
Unfortunately, the site provides little help to job-seekers
beyond attempting to sell visitors printed packages to
assist them in job searches. It does, however, contain links
to a number of other useful sites.

FedWorld Jobs

http://www.fedworld.gov/jobs/jobsearch.html
The database files at this Web site were created with input
from hundreds of human resources people in the federal
government. The database allows you to search abstracts
of open positions with the federal government, and it is
updated every Tuesday through Saturday at 9:30 A.M. EST.

USA Jobs

http://www.usajobs.opm.gov
The U.S. Office of Personnel Management runs a *huge*
jobs Web site at this address. All kinds of jobs are listed,
but a search feature makes it possible to easily find jobs
in the criminal justice area. Online applications are also
available.

CRIMINAL JUSTICE JOB-LISTING SERVICES

Criminal justice job-listing services come in two flavors: (1)
general and (2) agency- or area-specific. The following list
describes both kinds of services.

Corrections Jobs

http://database.corrections.com/career/jobs.asp
The Corrections Connection job-listing service. Allows
users to search for jobs by location, salary, and general
description.

Dr. Carlie's AdviseNet

http://www.smsu.edu/contrib/soc/advnet/advnet.htm
This site, a new concept in online advising for criminal
justice students, provides users with advice on where the
field is going, where to find jobs (includes many job
search engines), and additional useful information for students at *any* university. The site, maintained by Dr. Mike
Carlie of Southwest Missouri State University, was discussed in greater detail earlier in this chapter.

Ira Wilsker's Law Enforcement Employment Page

http://www.ih2000.net/ira/ira2.htm#jobs
This is an excellent, information-rich jobs page!

Law Enforcement Careers

http://www.gate.net/fcfjobs
This full-service career site is for those seeking employment in the law enforcement field. The site categorizes job
information as follows: (1) Federal Law Enforcement
Careers, (2) State Trooper Careers, and (3) Correctional
Officer Careers. The site also provides separate testing
guides, including one for federal law enforcement and one
for state and local law enforcement.

Law Enforcement Jobs

http://www.lawenforcementjobs.com
This may be the best site on the Web for anyone looking for
employment in the law enforcement field. The site lists jobs
with local departments, state departments, federal agencies,
the U.S. military, private security, associations, and schools.
A training calendar is an added bonus. The site, which is
free to job-seekers, allows you to post a résumé and cover
letter online and helps you manage your search online with
a Job Seeker Account. Résumés can be easily edited and
stay in the database until you delete them.

National Directory of Emergency Services
http://www1.policejobs.com/ndes/phome.html
This is an up-to-the-minute source for police department
employment opportunities.

Police Careers
http://www.policecareer.com/employment.html
A professional police résumé and career service company.
PoliceCareer.com is a national leader in law enforcement
pre-employment and promotional test preparation, career
books and résumé services.

Police Employment
http://www.policeemployment.com
This site provides information on careers in law enforcement and corrections and offers visitors the opportunity to
purchase law enforcement testing guides, videos, and
police interview guides. A jobs page shows "who is hiring."

Police Jobs
http://www.tap.net/hyslo/poljobs.htm
Here you will find an extensive list of police employment
sites.

The Police Officers' Internet Directory Jobs Page
http://www.officer.com/jobs.htm
This very comprehensive listing of current law enforcement jobs is highly recommended for those seeking law
enforcement employment.

The Public Safety Executive Association
http://www.policechief.com/default.htm
This membership site helps those who are beginning
careers in the field of public safety.

The State Police Information Center

http://www.internetwks.com/officers
This site is a nationwide provider of state and federal law
enforcement career information. The interface for this site
may be a bit tricky.

Job Information Sources by State

State and local job market and career information is available from state employment security agencies. These agencies develop detailed information about local labor markets, such as current and projected employment by occupation and industry, characteristics of the workforce, and changes in state and local economic activity. Listed in this appendix are mailing addresses and telephone numbers for the directors of research and analysis in these agencies. In most cases, Internet addresses for the agencies have also been provided.

ALABAMA

Chief, Labor Market Information
Alabama Department of Industrial Relations
649 Monroe St., Room 422
Montgomery, AL 36130
Phone: (334) 242-8800
Internet: http://www.dir.state.al.us/lmi

ALASKA

Chief, Research and Analysis
Alaska Department of Labor
P.O. Box 25501
Juneau, AK 99802-5501
Phone: (907) 465-4500
Internet: http://www.labor.state.ak.us

ARIZONA

Administrator, Research
Arizona Department of Economic Security
P.O. Box 6123, Site Code 733A
Phoenix, AZ 85005
Phone: (602) 542-3871
Internet:
http://www.de.state.az.us/links/economic/webpage/page6.html

ARKANSAS

Director, Labor Market Information
Arkansas Employment Security Department
P.O. Box 2981
Little Rock, AR 72203-2981
Phone: (501) 682-3159
Internet: http://www.state.ar.us/esd

CALIFORNIA

Chief, Labor Market Information Division
California Employment Development Department
P.O. Box 826880, MIC 57
Sacramento, CA 94280-0001
Phone: (916) 262-2160
Internet: http://www.calmis.cahwnet.gov

COLORADO

Director, Labor Market Information
Colorado Department of Labor and Employment
1515 Arapahoe St., Tower 2, Suite 400
Denver, CO 80202-2117
Phone: (303) 620-4977
Internet: http://lmi.cdle.state.co.us

CONNECTICUT

Director, Office of Research and Information
Connecticut Labor Department
200 Folly Brook Blvd.
Wethersfield, CT 06109-1114
Phone: (860) 263-6255
Internet: http://www.ctdol.state.ct.us/lmi/index.htm

DELAWARE

Director, Labor Market Information
Delaware Department of Labor
4425 North Market St.
Wilmington, DE 19802
Phone: (302) 761-8060
Internet: http://www.oolmi.net

DISTRICT OF COLUMBIA

Chief, Labor Market Information
District of Columbia Department of Employment Services
500 C St. N.W., Room 201
Washington, DC 20001
Phone: (202) 724-7214

FLORIDA

Bureau of Labor Market and Performance Information
Florida Department of Labor and Employment Security

2012 Capitol Circle S.E., Hartman Bldg., Suite 200
Tallahassee, FL 32399-2151
Phone: (850) 488-1048
Internet: http://lmi.floridajobs.org

GEORGIA

Director, Labor Market Information
Georgia Department of Labor
148 International Blvd. N.E.
Atlanta, GA 30303-1751
Phone: (404) 656-3177
Internet: http://www.dol.state.ga.us/lmi

GUAM

Administrator, Department of Labor
Guam Employment Services
P.O. Box 9970
Tamuning, GU 96931
Phone: (671) 475-0111
Internet: http://onestopcareer.gov.gu

HAWAII

Chief, Research and Statistics Office
Hawaii Department of Labor and Industrial Relations
830 Punchbowl St., Room 304
Honolulu, HI 96813
Phone: (808) 586-8999
Internet: http://dlir.state.hi.us

IDAHO

Bureau Chief, Research and Analysis
Idaho Department of Labor
317 Main St.
Boise, ID 83735-0001
Phone: (208) 334-6170
Internet: http://www.sde.state.id.us/cis

ILLINOIS

Manager, Economic Information and Analysis
Illinois Department of Employment Security
401 South State St., Suite 743
Chicago, IL 60605
Phone: (312) 793-2316
Internet: http://www.ioicc.state.il.us/LMI/default.htm

INDIANA

Director, Labor Market Information
Indiana Department of Workforce Development
Indiana Government Center, South, E211
10 North Senate Ave.
Indianapolis, IN 46204-2277
Phone: (317) 232-7460
Internet: http://www.dwd.state.in.us

IOWA

Administrator, Research and Information Services Division
Iowa Workforce Development
1000 East Grand Ave.
Des Moines, IA 50319-0209
Phone: (515) 281-6647
Internet: http://www.state.ia.us/iwd

KANSAS

Chief, Kansas Department of Human Resources
401 Southwest Topeka Blvd.
Topeka, KS 66603-3182
Phone: (785) 296-5058
Internet: http://entkdhr.ink.org/cgi-dir/newjob.cgi

KENTUCKY

Manager, LMI Branch, Division of Administration/Financial
Management
Kentucky Department of Employment Services
275 East Main St., Suite 2-C
Frankfort, KY 40621
Phone: (502) 564-7976
Internet:
http://www.des.state.ky.us/agencies/wforce/des/lmi/lmi.htm

LOUISIANA

Director, Research and Statistics Division
Louisiana Department of Labor
P.O. Box 94094
Baton Rouge, LA 70804-9094
Phone: (225) 342-3140
Internet: http://www.ldol.state.la.us/lmiqm.asp

MAINE

Director, Labor Market Information Services
Maine Department of Labor
20 Union St.
Augusta, ME 04330
Phone: (207) 287-2271
Internet: http://www.state.me.us/labor/lmis/frdef.htm

MARYLAND

Director, Office of Labor Market Analysis and Information
Maryland Department of Labor, Licensing, and Regulations
1100 North Eutaw St., Room 601
Baltimore, MD 21201
Phone: (410) 767-2250
Internet: http://www.dllr.state.md.us/lmi/index.htm

MASSACHUSETTS

Director, Labor Market Information and Research
Massachusetts Division of Employment and Training
19 Staniford St., 5th Floor
Boston, MA 02114
Phone: (617) 626-6560
Internet: http://www.detma.org/lmiinfo.htm

MICHIGAN

Director, Office of Labor Market Information
Michigan Jobs Commission, Employment Service Agency
7310 Woodward Ave., Room 520
Detroit, MI 48202
Phone: (313) 872-5904
Internet: http://www.michlmi.org

MINNESOTA

Director, BLS Programs, Research and Statistical Office
Minnesota Department of Economic Security
390 North Robert St.
St. Paul, MN 55104
Phone: (612) 296-4087
Internet: http://www.des.state.mn.us/lmi/careers

MISSISSIPPI

Director, Labor Market Information
Mississippi Employment Security Commission
P.O. Box 1699
Jackson, MS 39215-1699
Phone: (601) 961-7424
Internet: http://208.137.131.31/lmi

MISSOURI

Chief Administrator, Research and Analysis
Missouri Department of Labor and Industrial Relations
421 East Dunkin St.
P.O. Box 59
Jefferson City, MO 65104-0059
Phone: (573) 751-3637
Internet: http://www.works.state.mo.us/lmi

MONTANA

Director, Office of Research and Analysis
Montana Department of Labor and Industry
P.O. Box 1728
Helena, MT 59624-1728
Phone: (406) 444-2430; within Montana, (800) 633-0229; outside Montana, (800) 541-3904
Internet: http://rad.dli.state.mt.us

NEBRASKA

Administrator, Labor Market Information
Nebraska Department of Labor
550 South 16th St.
Lincoln, NE 68509-4600
Phone: (402) 471-9964
Internet: http://www.dol.state.ne.us/nelmi.htm

NEVADA

Chief, Bureau of Research and Analysis, Information Development and Processing Division
500 East Third St.
Carson City, NV 89713-0001
Phone: (775) 687-4550, ext. 228
Internet: http://www.state.nv.us/detr/lmi/index.htm

NEW HAMPSHIRE

Director, Economic and Labor Market Information Bureau
New Hampshire Department of Employment Security
32 South Main St.
Concord, NH 03301
Phone: (603) 228-4123
Internet: http://www.nhworks.state.nh.us/mlipage.htm

NEW JERSEY

Assistant Commissioner, Labor Planning and Analysis
New Jersey Department of Labor
P.O. Box 56, 5th Floor
Trenton, NJ 08625-0056
Phone: (609) 292-2643
Internet: http://www.state.nj.us/labor/lra

NEW MEXICO

Chief, Economic Research and Analysis Bureau
New Mexico Department of Labor
401 Broadway Blvd. N.E.
P.O. Box 1928
Albuquerque, NM 87103
Phone: (505) 841-8645
Internet: http://www3.state.nm.us/dol/dol_lmif.html

NEW YORK

Director, Division of Research and Statistics
New York Department of Labor
State Office Building Campus, Room 400
Albany, NY 12240
Phone: (518) 457-6369
Internet:
http://www.labor.state.ny.us/html/atool/lmiatool.htm

NORTH CAROLINA

Director, Labor Market Information
North Carolina Employment Security Commission
P.O. Box 25903
Raleigh, NC 27611
Phone: (919) 733-2936
Internet: http://www.esc.state.nc.us

NORTH DAKOTA

Manager, Program Support Area
North Dakota Job Service
1000 East Divide Ave.
P.O. Box 5507
Bismarck, ND 58506-5507
Phone: (701) 328-2868
Internet: http://www.state.nd.us/jsnd/lmi.htm

OHIO

Director, Labor Market Information Division
Ohio Bureau of Employment Services
145 South Front St.
P.O. Box 1618
Columbus, OH 43216-1618
Phone: (614) 752-9494
Internet: http://lmi.state.oh.us

OKLAHOMA

Director, Labor Market Information
Oklahoma Employment Security Commission
Will Rogers Memorial Office Bldg.
2401 North Lincoln
Oklahoma City, OK 73105
Phone: (405) 525-7265
Internet: http://www.oesc.state.ok.us/lmi/default.htm

OREGON

Director, Labor Market Information
Oregon Employment Department
875 Union St. N.E.
Salem, OR 97311
Phone: (503) 947-1212
Internet: http://olmis.emp.state.or.us

PENNSYLVANIA

Director, Bureau of Research and Statistics
Pennsylvania Department of Labor and Industry
Seventh and Forester Sts., Room 101
Harrisburg, PA 17120-0001
Phone: (717) 787-3266
Internet: http://www.lmi.state.pa.us

PUERTO RICO

Director, Research and Statistics Division
Puerto Rico Bureau of Employment Security
505 Munoz Rivera Ave., 20th Floor
Hato Rey, PR 00918
Phone: (787) 754-5385

RHODE ISLAND

Director, Labor Market Information
Rhode Island Department of Employment and Training
101 Friendship St.
Providence, RI 02903-3740
Phone: (401) 222-3730
Internet: http://www.dlt.state.ri.us/webdev/lmi

SOUTH CAROLINA

Director, Labor Market Information
South Carolina Employment Security Commission
610 Hampton St.
P.O. Box 995
Columbia, SC 29202
Phone: (803) 737-2660
Internet: http://www.sces.org/lmi/index.htm

SOUTH DAKOTA

Director, Labor Market Center
South Dakota Department of Labor
P.O. Box 4730
Aberdeen, SD 57402-4730
Phone: (605) 626-2314
Internet: http://www.state.sd.us/dol/lmic/index.htm

TENNESSEE

Director, Research and Statistics Division
Tennessee Department of Employment Security
Davy Crockett Tower, 11th Floor
500 James Robertson Pkwy.
Nashville, TN 37245-1000
Phone: (615) 741-2284
Internet: http://www.state.tn.us/labor-wfd/outlooks/select.htm

TEXAS

Director, Labor Market Information
Texas Workforce Commission
9001 North IH-35, Suite 103A
Austin, TX 78778
Phone: (512) 491-4802
Internet: http://www.twc.state.tx.us/lmi/lmi.html

UTAH

Director, Labor Market Information
Utah Department of Workforce Services
140 East 300 S.
P.O. Box 45249
Salt Lake City, UT 84145-0249
Phone: (801) 526-9401
Internet: http://www.dws.state.ut.us

VERMONT

Research and Analysis
Vermont Department of Employment and Training
5 Green Mountain Dr.
P.O. Box 488
Montpelier, VT 05601-0488
Phone: (802) 828-4153
Internet: http://www.det.state.vt.us

VIRGINIA

Director, Economic Information and Services Division
Virginia Employment Commission
703 East Main St.
P.O. Box 1358
Richmond, VA 23218-1358
Phone: (804) 786-7496
Internet: http://www.vec.state.va.us/lbrmkt/lmi.htm

VIRGIN ISLANDS

Chief, Bureau of Labor Statistics
Virgin Islands Department of Labor
53A and 54B Kronprindsens Gade
Charlotte Amalie, St. Thomas, VI 00820
Phone: (340) 776-3700

WASHINGTON

Director, Labor Market and Economic Analysis
Employment Security Division
Mail Stop 6000
P.O. Box 9046
Olympia, WA 98507-9046
Phone: (360) 438-4804
Internet: http://www.wa.gov/esd/lmea

WEST VIRGINIA

Director, Research, Information, and Analysis
West Virginia Bureau of Employment Programs
112 California Ave.
Charleston, WV 25305-0112
Phone: (304) 558-2660
Internet: http://www.state.wv.us/bep/lmi/default.htm

WISCONSIN

Chief, LMI Data Development
Wisconsin Department of Workforce Development
201 East Washington Ave., Room 2214
Madison, WI 53702
Phone: (608) 266-2930
Internet: http://www.dwd.state.wi.us/dwelmi

WYOMING

Manager, Research and Planning, Division of Administration
Wyoming Department of Employment
P.O. Box 2760
Casper, WY 82602-2760
Phone: (307) 473-3801
Internet: http://wydoe.state.wy.us

Index